Los Angeles & SOUTHERN CALIFORNIA

by Taj Bates

This book is for those
to whom California is still
an unseen and fabulous land
of sunshine, oranges and wonder.

And for those curious for
something new and little-known
about the everyday California
in which they live, work and play.

Prologue

Have you ever noticed how most every travel guide opens with a brief rundown of the top 10, 15 or 25 things to do in a country or the like... followed by a data dump of hundreds of places you'll never have the time nor inclination to visit in your lifetime?

Well, you won't find anything like that in this guide. Why?

Because this entire book is a curated collection of Los Angeles and Southern California's Must Sees, Must Dos and Must Eats.

Written by a Californian and world traveller, it is a fab mix of iconic places you've heard of, but will see in a new and fascinating light, alongside off-the-beaten-path experiences you'll never forget.

Each chapter delves into a YOLO-worthy (*You Only Live Once*) destination like the Venice Boardwalk or Disneyland... gives you the details and insider tips you need to have an amazing time while you're there... and highlights awesome things to do and places to eat nearby.

And the best part?

This guidebook is tailor-made For You. Whether you're a fastidious planner; someone who likes to 'wing it' on-the-go; or somewhere in between.

With The YOLO Guide in hand, you are destined to have a fun and fabulous adventure in America's Dreamiest State. *Bon voyage!*

*We're a land of discovery.
We're not chained to
any form of history
or a past.*

We chill like that.

— Roy Choi

YOLO Cali!

Ah, Southern California... A golden land of bodacious beaches, poetic deserts, snowy mountains and fertile valleys ripe with all manner of *fruits de la terre*.

At its heart is Los Angeles, the *City of Angels* and the *Creative Capital of the World*. LA is the second largest metropolis in the U.S., and its sun-kissed, urban sprawl is overflowing with art, culture and innovation—from the film sets and red carpets of Hollywood; to the murals and music halls of Downtown LA (DTLA); to the museums and surf havens of West LA.

Two hours east of LA is Palm Springs and the Coachella Valley, home to golf courses, casinos, mid-century architecture, natural mineral pools and the largest desert fan palm oasis in the world.

Thirty to sixty minutes south of LA is Orange County, the 'OC,' a land of glistening yachts, plein-air shopping malls, multi-million dollar beach homes and highways abuzz with fans and families en route to Disneyland, the *Happiest Place on Earth*.

And two to three hours south of LA is the county of San Diego, a metropolitan paradise with perfect weather; laid-back beach towns; and gorgeous bays traversed by mammoth aircraft carriers sailing to and fro the largest U.S. Navy base on the West Coast.

As you venture to one or more of these destinations, you will gain a rich and profound appreciation for what makes SoCal such a unique and YOLO-worthy place to explore and to *just be*.

Los Angeles

Annual Festivals & Events	2
Eatin' Good in LA	5
Gourmet Food Trucks	9
Certified Farmers Markets	12

Hollywood

Live Sitcom Taping	15
Hollywood Boulevard	21
Hollywood Bowl	31
Hollywood Sign	41
The Magic Castle	49

West LA

Venice Boardwalk	57
Getty Museum	65
La Brea Tar Pits	75

Downtown LA

Mural Capital of the World — 81

Space Shuttle Endeavour — 89

Walt Disney Concert Hall — 95

Southern Cali

Annual Festivals & Events — 106

Eatin' Good in SoCal — 110

Certified Farmers Markets — 112

Disneyland — 115

Indian Canyon Oases — 127

North County, San Diego — 137

Annual Festivals & Events

 ## Tournament of Roses

The Tournament of Roses is a century-old tradition and televised event that begins with the Rose Parade in the morning—replete with marching bands, performers and ornate floats decorated with roses—followed by the Rose Bowl college football championship, when the nation's best college teams face off against each other.

Rose Parade: curbside viewing is free and first-come; grandstand seating is $50-$95+, available online in Feb (year before) • Rose Bowl: ticket prices vary; available online in early Dec • TournamentofRoses.com/events • 1001 Rose Bowl Dr, Pasadena

 ## Academy Awards

For nearly 90 years, the Academy Awards has reigned supreme as Hollywood's biggest and most glamorous event—where who won is just as important as "who are you wearing." Via the Oscars Red Carpet Fan Experience, you could win a golden ticket to stand in a bleacher section overlooking the red carpet, where you will be able to see Tinseltown's biggest stars up close and in living color.

Free! • Enter the Fan Experience drawing in early Dec: Oscars.org/enter • 6801 Hollywood Blvd

An Indonesia-inspired float decked out with fresh flowers at the Rose Parade

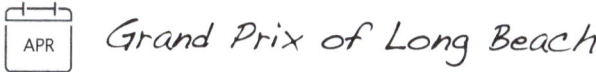

| APR | *Grand Prix of Long Beach* |

Every spring, the Long Beach waterfront transforms into a 1.968 mi (3.167 km) racetrack where fast and furious IndyCars race upwards of 230+ mph (370 kph) for the win... Formula DRIFT drivers leave plumes of smoke in their tire-screeching wake... and amped up 'super trucks' leap into the air like Bambis on Red Bull.

1-Day pass $30-$87+, 3-Day pass $85-$142+; purchasable via GPLB.com starting in Sept • Cedar Ave & Bay St, Long Beach

| SEPT | *LA County Fair* |

Have you ever seen a curly-haired pig? Well, at the LA County Fair, the largest in the state, you can see all manner of farm animals; try artery-clogging foods like deep fried cheeseburgers

Creepy Jack-in-the-boxes at the WEHO Halloween Carnaval • IndyCars racing 'round the bend at the Grand Prix of Long Beach

and deep fried apple pie; watch circus acrobats and marching bands; rock out to headliners like Chaka Khan, ZZ Top and The Beach Boys; and enjoy 70+ carnival rides and games.

Admission $14 (Mon-Fri), $20 (Sat-Sun), Season Pass $29 • LACF.com • 1101 West McKinley Ave, Pomona

OCT | WEHO Halloween Carnaval

Get *dressed to the fangs* in your fiercest costume and revel in the world's largest Halloween street party, which takes place smack dab in the LGBT mecca of West Hollywood, where you can go on a haunted pub crawl; rock out to live DJs and artists like Daft Punk and Boy George; and dance with drag queens into the wee hours of the morn!

Free! • Oct 31, 6pm-11pm • VisitWestHollywood.com/halloween-carnaval • Santa Monica Blvd & North San Vicente Blvd

Eatin' Good in LA!

LA County is the birthplace of the California roll, Cobb salad, Valencia orange, Sriracha sauce and the smoothie. It is where the modern fro-yo craze took off in 2005. And it is the purveyor of...

Gourmet Pizza

There once was a time when putting fancy ingredients on a pizza was a fanciful idea, indeed. But that all changed in 1982 when Wolfgang Puck opened Spago, debuting a 'casual fine dining' concept that revolutionized modern dining to be less stuffy and more laid-back and intimate...

Which gave rise to Spago's second innovation—the California-style pizza, a gourmet pizza topped with a creative mix of artisan ingredients. If you like salmon, you should definitely try its signature pizza—of house-smoked salmon, dill *creme fraiche* and caviar—which is always a hit at the Oscars' official after-party.

> SPAGO IS 'ONE OF LA'S 10 BEST RESTAURANTS' – *LOS ANGELES TIMES*

$35-$270+ • ☑ Reservations • You can always order a pizza, even when they're not on the menu! • Mon, 6pm-10pm; Tue-Sat, noon-2:30pm & 6pm-close; Sun, 5:30pm-10pm • (310) 385-0880 • 176 North Canon Dr

Korexican Cuisine

LA is home to the largest Mexican and Korean commuinties outside of Mexico and Korea, so it was only a matter of time before the two cultures merged in a culinary way.

Chef and Kogi BBQ Truck founder, Roy Choi, popularized Korexican-style street food during LA's gourmet food truck revolution in the late 2000s. Since then, he has opened several restaurants, including Kogi Taqueria, which serves up Korexican fusions like kimchi quesadillas and carnitas tacos with Korean BBQ sauce.

$5-$10+ • Tue-Sat, 11am-11pm; Sun, 11am-9pm • (424) 326-3031 • Metro Rail: Palms (Expo line), plus 6 block walk • 3500 Overland Ave

French-Dip Sandwich

LA has a Chinatown, a Koreatown... and it used to have a French Town, in the early 1900s, that was home to Basque immigrants from southern France.

Today, the only remnant of its existence is Philippe the Original, a 100-year-old deli that keeps a French Town tradition alive in the form of the French-dip—a roast beef sandwich on a French roll, dipped in *au jus*—that first came to be at this very deli in 1918.

$10+ • 6am-10pm • For a spicy kick, get their specialty hot mustard on the side • (213) 628-3781 • Metro Rail: Union Station (gold, purple, red), plus 3 block walk • 1001 North Alameda St

Animal-Style Cheeseburger

LA County is where the first cheesburger was grilled, in the 1920s, and where the first drive-thru burger stand—an In-N-Out Burger—opened in 1948. Since then, In-N-Out has grown into a chain with 300+ locations and an army of zealouts who herald it *the best burger place in all the land*.

A fan favorite is the Animal-Style Cheeseburger, an off-menu item that boasts a mustard-grilled beef patty (or patties!) topped with fresh lettuce and tomato, pickles, grilled onions, melted American cheese and a special sauce, all on a fresh-baked bun.

In-N-Out near LAX: $5-$10+; 10:30am-1am; 9149 South Sepulveda Blvd. This location is a popular pit stop to/fro the airport. It's often crazy crowded, but the seating area overlooks a runway so you can watch planes landing whilst wolfing down your burger! • In-N-Out.com/locations

Hass Avocado

California does not have an official state fruit, but if it did, it would likely be the Hass avocado (like its soulmate, tomato, avocado is very much a fruit).

All the world's Hass avocados can trace their roots back to a seedling planted on an LA County hobby orchard in 1926. Today, 90 percent of the avocados grown in the U.S. are of the Hass variety, and the vast majority of them are harvested in SoCal (San Diego County is the 'Avocado Capital of the World').

Because avocados are so plentiful here, Southern Californians put it in or on pretty much everything—burgers, salads, pizzas, omelets, sushi, sandwiches, cakes, and, of course, guacamole.

So do as the locals do… stop by a Certified Farmers Market (p 12) and get some farm fresh avocados to add to your next meal.

YOLO-a-Go-Go Guacamole!

Whenever I'm roadtripping in California, this recipe is often my go-to after a long hike, drive or day of sightseeing: *TheYOLOGuide.com/guacamole*.

It is hearty and delicious; quick 'n easy to make; and calls for only a handful of ingredients that all travel quite well.

Gourmet Food Trucks

Eat street food the LA way by partaking of the savories n' sweets in food trucks that roam the City of Angels, where the global, gourmet food truck craze first took flight in the late 2000s.

Get the biggest bang for your tastebuds by attending a food truck rally, where a bunch of food trucks congregate in a lot or on a block, offering up a delightful array of delectable dishes.

On Saturdays, May thru October, you can enjoy the best of multiple worlds—food truck rally; live music; and an outdoor screening of a film like *Back to the Future*—when you attend a StreetFoodCinema.com or EatSeeHear.com event.

★ *Arrive early; rallies can get crowded on evenings and weekends.*

★ *Bring cash; some vendors do not take credit cards.*

★ *Follow @TheYOLOGuide on Twitter and subscribe to our LA Food Trucks list to view real-time tweets from the city's best food trucks on where they'll be dropping anchor next.*

Hollywood

Monday	5:30pm-8pm, generally	**On the Lot in Los Feliz** 2060 North Vermont Ave *3 mi / 5 km from Hollywood Boulevard*
Thursday	5:30pm-9:30pm	**NOHO Food Truck Collective** 5211 Tujunga Ave *6 mi / 9.5 km from Hollywood Boulevard*

West LA

Mon-Fri	10:30am-2:30pm	**Food Truck Alley** 2700 Pennsylvania Ave, Santa Monica *4.2 mi / 6.8 km from Venice Boardwalk* *5.5 mi / 8.8 km from Getty Center*
Tuesday	11am-3pm	**Gateway to Go by LAX Airport** 6101 West 98th St *7.5 mi / 12 km from Venice Boardwalk*
	4:30pm-9:30pm	**Santa Monica Food Truck Lot** 2612 Main St, Santa Monica *1.4 mi / 2.3 km from Venice Boardwalk* *6 mi / 9.5 km from Getty Villa*
Friday	5pm-10pm (1st Fri only)	**The Brig Lot in Venice** 1515 Abbot Kinney Blvd *0.8 mi / 1.3 km from Venice Boardwalk*

Downtown LA

Tue-Thu	11am-2pm	**Grand Park ¡Lunchtime!** 200 North Grand Ave *0.1 mi	230 m from Disney Concert Hall*
Mon & Fri	11am-2pm	**Pershing Square in DTLA** 532 South Olive St *0.5 mi	850 m from Disney Concert Hall*

Certified Farmers Markets

Once upon a time ago, Los Angeles was covered with citrus groves, fruit orchards, vegetable fields and *rancheros*.

Today, while you would be hard-presssed to find a large farm in LA's urban sprawl, California is still the most agriculturally-rich state in the U.S., where a veritable *Who's Who* of produce, nuts, flowers and honey are harvested under the California sun.

In LA, you can savor this harvest at a Certified Farmers Market (CFM), where you can bite into fruits and veggies fresh from a local farm; discover delectable eats and treats by local chefs; and take home unique finds crafted by local artists and artisans.

★ *Bring cash; some vendors do not accept credit cards.*

★ *Bring a reusable bag or two to carry all of your goodies in.*

★ *Arrive early so you'll have first dibs on the best produce.*

Hollywood

Sunday	8am-1pm	**Hollywood CFM** 1600 Ivar Ave *1 mi l 1.5 km from Hollywood Boulevard*
	10am-2pm	**Melrose Place CFM** 8400 Melrose Ave *3 mi l 3 km from Hollywood Boulevard*

West LA

Wed & Sat	8:30am-1pm, generally	**Downtown Santa Monica CFM** Arizona Ave & 2nd St, Santa Monica *3 mi l 4.5 km from Venice Boardwalk* *5 mi l 8 km from Getty Villa*
Wednesday	11am-3pm, generally	**Miracle Mile CFM** 5700 Wilshire Blvd *0.1 mi l 190 m from La Brea Tarpits*
Thursday	10am-2pm	**Century City CFM** 10100 Santa Monica Blvd *5 mi l 8 km from Getty Center*
Sunday	8am–1pm	**Pacific Palisades CFM** 1037 Swarthmore Ave *3.5 mi l 5.5 km from Getty Villa*

Sunday	8:30am–1pm	**Downtown Santa Monica CFM** 2640 Main St, Santa Monica *1.5 mi / 2 km from Venice Boardwalk*
	9am–1pm	**Beverly Hills CFM** 9300 Civic Center Dr, Beverly Hills *3 mi / 5 km from La Brea Tarpits*
	9am-2:30pm	**Brentwood CFM** 741 Gretna Green Way *3.4 mi / 5.5 km from Getty Center*

Downtown LA

Wednesday	10am-2pm	**Pershing Square CFM** 532 South Olive St *0.6 mi / 900 m from Disney Concert Hall*
	11am–3pm	**Univ. of Southern California CFM** 3415 South Figueroa St *0.5 mi / 1 km from Endeavour Shuttle*
Thursday	10am-2pm	**FIG at 7th CFM** 735 South Figueroa St *1 mi / 1.5 km from Disney Concert Hall*
Friday	10am-2pm	**Downtown LA CFM** 333 South Hope St *0.5 mi / 1 km from Disney Concert Hall*

Live Sitcom Taping

Los Angeles is where sitcoms were first taped in front of a live studio audience — during the inaugural taping of 'I Love Lucy' in 1951 — and it is still the best place to get a behind-the-scenes look at the making of a half-hour sitcom.

Planning Guide

If you have a favorite TV sitcom, there is a good chance it was taped on a studio lot in or near Hollywood, where live sitcoms tapings have been a mainstay for nearly 70 years!

Tickets to sitcom tapings are free and can be reserved online generally 30 days in advance via:

TVTickets.com

On-Camera-Audiences.com

TVTix.com

Popular TV shows like *The Big Bang Theory* sell out pretty quickly, so it is best to reserve those the moment they are available.

Insider Tips

★ Live sitcom tapings are definitely fun and insightful, but they also require a time commitment of 4 to 5 hours and you are expected to stay the entire time.

★ Most ticket distributors overbook their shows, so your seat is not guaranteed. Check the fine print on your ticket to determine whether your seat is guaranteed. If not...

★ Seats are filled on a first-come basis, so it is best to arrive 60+ minutes early to get a seat closer to the stage.

★ On the day of your reservation, be sure to bring a printed copy of your ticket to the studio lot where the show is taped.

★ Before the taping starts, a local comedian will serve as a 'warm up act' to get the audience laughing and clapping. Then the cast and crew will be introduced, during which some of the members of the cast will often chat with the audience for a bit until the director yells, "places everyone!"

★ Most likely, during the course of the taping, the warm up comedian will give away signed t-shirts, DVDs, gift cards and the like. But this will require some form of participation on your part, so be prepared to be silly and game for anything!

★ DO eat a good meal beforehand. Though most shows will feed you something—some a sandwich and a cookie, others just a lame muffin—it will not be substantive or sustaining.

★ DO NOT bring a cell phone or camera. They are not allowed beyond the parking lot and should remain in your car.

★ DO bring a hat for shade and a book or magazine to read while you wait in line, usually outdoors, to be ushered to the studio soundstage. Also, bring a jacket in case the soundstage is cold.

★ For most tapings, you must be age 18+. For shows targeted to kids, the minimum age can be as low as 10.

On set with the 'The Big Bang Theory' cast • Cruising past soundstages and production offices during the Warner Bros. Studio Tour

Notable Nearby

The Ellen DeGeneres Show
See some of Hollywood's biggest stars dance, chit chat and play goofy games with host, Ellen DeGeneres, during a taping of this daytime talk show filmed on the Warner Bros. studio lot. You may even get a chance to go on stage to play or dance along!

Free tickets can be reserved on EllenTV.com/tickets 1-3 months in advance. Limited standby tickets available day-of by calling (818) 954-5929 before noon • Must be age 14+ • Reserve 'Guaranteed Tickets' so you do not have to stand in line for hours for a good seat • Gate 3: 4301 W Olive Ave, Burbank

Warner Bros. Studio Tour
During a 2-hour guided tour, you will get to sit in Central Perk Cafe from the set of *Friends*; view props, cars and costumes from

iconic films; and star in an actual movie scene via the magic of green screen.

Tickets $62; via WBStudioTour.com • Tours depart every 15 minutes, 8am-4pm, generally • (877) 492-8687 • Parking $7 • Gate 6: 3400 Warner Blvd, Burbank

'Extra' Live at Universal Studios Hollywood

See host Mario Lopez in all his dimpled glory as he interviews fellow celebrities during a live taping of *Extra*, a newstainment show shot in front of the Universal Studios Hollywood theme park.

Live tapings occur at varying intervals Mon-Fri, 10am-4pm, at the Universal globe water fountain • You can view a schedule of upcoming celebrity guests on ExtraTV.com/at-universal-studios-hollywood • Parking $2-$35; 2-hour parking is $2 with validation from a Universal CityWalk store or restaurant • Metro Rail: Universal City / Studio City (red); plus free shuttle bus to the park every 10-15 min • 100 Universal City Plaza, Universal City

Studio Tour at Universal Studios Hollywood

Universal Studios is where the idea of a studio tour was born—in 1915, during the Silent Movie era, when tours cost only 25 cents ($6 today). The tour died off during the advent of *Talkies*, but was resurrected in 1965 to the delight of movie fans from near and afar. Over time, crowd-pleasing stunts and special effects were added to the tour, which became so popular, it spawned the creation of the Universal Studios Hollywood theme park.

1-Day Park Admission $105+ (includes access to the Studio Tour). Skip long lines by purchasing tickets and a parking pass online: UniversalStudiosHollywood.com • Park hours vary and are posted online • You can splurge for the VIP Experience ($329+), which includes a VIP studio tour, front of the line access to every ride, valet parking, breakfast and lunch • (800) UNIVERSAL • Metro Rail: Universal City / Studio City (red); plus free shuttle bus to the park every 10-15 min • Parking $18+ • 100 Universal City Plaza, Universal City

Take a walk down cinema lane via this iconic boulevard of movie palaces, celebrity handprints and Walk of Fame stars that has played host to the glitz n' glam of Hollywood for over a century.

3 Ways to Go Hollywood on the Boulevard

Grauman's Chinese Theatre

This opulent theatre was built in 1927 under the tutelage of Sid Grauman, a movie theatre mogul and marketing genius who was the mastermind behind two Hollywood traditions: the red carpet movie premiere; and the practice of memorializing a star's handprints and footprints in the theatre's forecourt.

Nowadays, you can high-five the handprints of your favorite movie stars in the forecourt. And with luck and planning, you can even see the stars of today during movie premieres and handprint ceremonies that are held here a few times every month.

You can also watch the latest blockbuster movie in the theatre's main auditorium, which is wondrously ornate and boasts a new IMAX screen over which the theatre's original red and gold silk curtain still hangs.

> *Movies $18-$20 • 8am-midnight • 30-minute guided tour: $13.50; tours conducted 10:15am-6pm, generally • Movie tickets can be purchased on-site or via TCLChineseTheatres.com • (323) 461-3331 • Metro Rail: Hollywood / Highland (red), plus 1 block walk • 6925 Hollywood Blvd*

Grauman's Egyptian Theatre

The Egyptian Theatre is the first great movie palace Sid Grauman built on Hollywood Boulevard back in 1922. Though not as well known as its younger sibling, the Chinese Theatre, the Egyptian has its own unique charm.

You can watch a classic film in its lavishly Pharaonic auditorium where films are shown a few days each week. Also, if your travel dates align, you can join an insightful, behind-the-scenes tour that takes place once a month, usually on a Saturday morning.

> *Movies $11 • 1-hour guided tour: $7-$10 • AmericanCinematheque.com/egyptian/egypt.htm • (323) 461-2020 • Metro Rail: Hollywood / Highland (red), plus 2 block walk • 6712 Hollywood Blvd*

Hollywood Roosevelt Hotel Lobby & Pool

Step back in time and experience what it must have been like to sit in the lobby or by the pool of this historic hotel during Hollywood's Golden Age, when Clark Gable, Greta Garbo, Errol

Flynn and Marilyn Monroe graced its Spanish tile floors.

Built in 1927, and financed in part by Sid Grauman, the hotel played host to the very first Academy Awards in 1929. Its lobby is a lovely place to enjoy a classic cocktail or glass of wine amidst a swanky interior brimming with Spanish, Moorish and Roman architectural influences.

As an added respite from the bustle of the Boulevard, you can escape to the hotel's heated pool and plush loungers, where you do not have to be a hotel guest to take a refreshing dip.

> *Cocktails $15+; bar service 11:30am-2am • Non-hotel guest pool access: noon (12pm) till midnight. To commandeer a poolside lounger, you must spend a minimum of $50 per person on food and drink from the pool bar, Mon-Fri; $100 per person, Sat-Sun • (323) 856-1970 • Metro Rail: Hollywood / Highland (red), plus 2 block walk • 7000 Hollywood Blvd*

Planning Guide

If you are looking for the center of the action on Hollywood Boulevard, look no further than the 6800 and 6900 blocks, where the Chinese Theatre is located.

This is where most of the costumed actors—dressed as Yoda, Superman, Captain Sparrow, Marilyn Monroe and the like—hang out for photo ops with tourists. It is also where you can:

Tour the Dolby Theatre, home of the annual Academy Awards

(tours are pricey, however, at $22 for just 30 minutes); listen to a pre-movie serenade of Disney tunes being played on a near century-old pipe organ in the El Capitan Theatre, which Sid Grauman built in 1926; and, of course, go hunting for your favorite entertainers' stars on the Hollywood Walk of Fame.

More Info	(323) 467-6412
Parking	$2-$15 at the Hollywood & Highland shopping complex (address below). First 2 hours are $2 with validation from participating shops and restaurants, as well as the Visitor Information Center located in the courtyard outside of the Dolby Theatre.
Metro Rail	Hollywood / Highland (red)
Map It	6801 Hollywood Blvd

Insider Tips

★ The best time to stroll along the Walk of Fame and the Chinese Theatre forecourt is early in the morning, before the crowds descend. The forecourt opens at 8am.

★ Via WalkofFame.com, you can search for the geographic location of your favorite entertainers' stars on the Walk; and view dates and honorees for upcoming Walk of Fame dedication ceremonies, which are free and open to the public.

★ The best time to see the costumed characters is after noon (12pm), any day of the week. If you take a photo with one

Jimmy Kimmel (left) and prima ballerina Misty Copeland (center) during a skit on Jimmy Kimmel Live! • Kermits hanging out on the Hollywood Walk of Fame

of them, it is customary to give a tip of at least $1.

★ Do you love to people watch? Then perch yourself on a bench outside the Dolby Theatre where you can watch an entertaining parade of tourists; street hawkers; and costumed actors as they slip in and out of character with the ebb and flow of the crowd. (Just be mentally prepared in case you spy Superman taking a cigarette break!)

★ If you are a TV fanatic, every March, the Dolby Theatre hosts PaleyFest, a 2-week festival of nightly panels during which you can see and hear from the writers and actors behind your favorite TV shows like *Scandal* and *The Big Bang Theory*. Tickets are $30-$80+; via Media.PaleyCenter.org.

★ In September, the Paley Center for Media hosts Fall TV Previews in Beverly Hills (5 mi | 8 km away), during which you can attend screenings of upcoming TV shows with cast and writers in attendance. Tickets: Media.PaleyCenter.org.

Notable Nearby

Jimmy Kimmel Live!
(70 ft / 21 m away)
Get up close and personal with a bona fide movie star during a taping of this late night talk show, which is filmed on the Boulevard, inside a Masonic temple built in 1921.

Free! Tickets reservable on 1iota.com 1 month in advance. • Must be age 18+ • Arrive 30-60 minutes early to guarantee a seat. Eat beforehand, tapings can last 3+ hours. • Metro Rail: Hollywood / Highland (red) • 6840 Hollywood Blvd

Rooftop Film Club
(0.9 mi / 1.5 km away)
Watch an old school or new school film—like *Clueless*, *Blade Runner*, *The Goonies*, *Grease* or *Ghostbusters*—atop the Ricardo Montalban Theatre, right in the heart of Hollywood.

Screenings: Tue-Sat (Apr-Oct) • Tickets $19+ via RooftopCinemaClub.com/LA • Arrive early to snag good seats; be prepared for 5 flights of stairs • Must be age 18+ • Metro Rail: Hollywood / Vine (red), plus 2 block walk • 1615 Vine St

Skybar
(2.3 mi / 3.6 km away)
Have lunch and a dip in the pool at this open-air bar with fantastic views of West Hollywood and beyond. Or come later in the day for a breathtaking sunset. At night, the bar often pulses with live music by local bands and DJs. And in summer (June-Oct), it hosts Dive In Theater screenings of fan favorites like *Casino Royale*.

Open to non-hotel guests 1pm-2am; pool accessible till 5pm • Wine & cocktails $13+; bar menu $15+ • Upcoming events: BackofHouse.morganshotelgroup.

com • (323) 848-6025 • Atop the Mondrian Hotel: 8440 Sunset Blvd

Pantages Theatre
(0.8 mi / 1.3 km km away)
Get your Broadway fix at this Art Deco theatre that is the last of the great movie palaces built on the Boulevard. It opened to great fanfare in 1930 and, throughout the 1950s, was the official home of the Academy Awards. Nowadays, it is the official home of traveling Broadway shows like *Wicked* and *Hamilton*.

Ticket prices vary; purchasable via HollywoodPantages.com • Must be age 5+ to attend • (800) 982-2787 • Parking $10-$20+ in private lots nearby • Metro Rail: Hollywood / Vine (red) • 6233 Hollywood Blvd

Melrose Trading Post
(2.5 mi / 4 km away)
You never know what you'll find at this eclectic outdoor market that boasts 200+ vendors selling a variety of wares—art, antiques, furniture, clothing, jewelry and more. Plus, food and live music.

Sun, 9am-5pm • Admission $3 (cash only) • Free valet parking at corner of Fairfax Ave and Clinton St • 7850 Melrose Ave

Dining Nearby

25 Degrees
(0.1 mi / 180 m away)
American ◆ Breakfast, burgers, fries, milkshakes, onion rings, salad
$20-$30+ • Open 24/7 • (323) 785-7244 • 7000 Hollywood Blvd

Bossa Nova on Sunset

(0.8 mi / 1 km away)
Brazilian ◆ Salad, sandwiches, pizza, carne, seafood, steak
$20-$30+ • Sun-Wed, 11am-3:30am; Thu-Sat, 11am-4am • (323) 436-7999
• *7181 Sunset Blvd*

The Griddle Cafe

(1.5 mi / 2.5 km away)
American ◆ Breakfast, burgers, salads, sandwiches, tacos
$15-$20+ • Mon-Fri, 7am-4pm; Sat-Sun, 8am-4pm • (323) 874-0377 • *7916 Sunset Blvd*

Grub

(1.5 mi / 2 km away)
American ◆ Brunch, burgers, pasta, salad, sandwiches, soup, carne
$20-30+ • Mon-Thu, 11am-9pm; Fri, 11am-10pm, Sat, 9am-3pm & 5pm-10pm; Sun, 9am-3pm & 5pm-9pm • (323) 461-3663 • *911 Seward St*

Musso & Frank Grill

(0.3 mi / 400 m away)

> FOUNDED IN 1919, THIS IS THE OLDEST RESTAURANT IN HOLLYWOOD

Steakhouse ◆ Breakfast, pasta, salad, carne, seafood, steak
$25-$55+ • ☑ Reservations • Tue-Sat, 11am-11pm; Sun, 4pm-9pm • (323) 467-7788 • *6667 Hollywood Blvd*

Roscoe's House of Chicken & Waffles

(1 mi / 2 km away)
American ◆ Breakfast, fried chicken, waffles, sweet potato pie
$15-$25+ • Mon-Thu, 8:30am-midnight; Fri-Sat, 8am-4am; Sun, 8am-midnight
• (323) 466-7453 • *1514 North Gower St*

Hollywood Bowl

Enjoy a concert under the stars at this, the largest natural amphitheatre in the country, where you can rock out with music's biggest superstars or ride on a wave of nostalgia as the LA Philharmonic plays crowd-pleasing scores from cult films and Broadway classics.

Planning Guide

Witnessesing Angelenos as they converge upon the Hollywood Bowl—bearing blankets, seat cushions, wine, picnic baskets and even LED candles—you would think they were headed to an elaborate and nostalgic slumber party.

This, my friend, is what makes the Bowl extra special. It is a near century-old amphitheatre wherein you can enjoy the comforts of home amidst natural beauty and world-class music.

You can catch a concert at the Bowl during its official season, June thru September, which boasts a range of musical genres to choose from, as well as fun pop symphony concerts like *Bugs Bunny at the Symphony* and *Star Wars in Concert*. Some shows even feature fireworks, which is a special treat.

More Info	HollywoodBowl.com	(323) 850-2000
Price	$1-$100+
Parking	$18-$50+, stacked parking only (no early exit)
Metro Rail + Bus	Hollywood / Highland (red), plus the $6 Bowl Shuttle from the Hollywood & Highland Orange Court (on Orange Dr, just north of Hollywood Blvd). The shuttle is free if you show your LA Metro TAP card; it departs every 10-15 minutes, beginning 2.5 hours before showtime. Alternatively, you can walk 1 mi (1.6 km) from the station to the Bowl.
Map It	2301 North Highland Ave

Tickets are available starting in early May. I highly suggest purchasing your tickets then, as the best seats as well as the cheapest seats (for less than $10) get snatched up very quickly.

The Bowl also hosts lease concerts headlined by big name artists, May-Oct. These shows are ad hoc and usually more expensive.

Seating Guide

Via HollywoodBowl.com/seating, you can check out the view from each of the following sections:

Box Seats *Pool Circle, Garden, Terrace*

- Front and center to the stage
- Wood-partitioned boxes with collapsible canvas chairs and folding tables; accommodates 4-6 people
- Most expensive; upwards of $100+ for official Bowl events
- Note: For most lease events, the Pool Circle has rows of metal chairs instead of boxes

Super Seats *Sections G1, H, J1*

- In the center of the amphitheatre, behind the box seats
- Stadium-style plastic seats with built-in cup holders
- Mid-range; a great deal for the view and proximity you get

Bench Seats

Sections D-F3, G2, J2-X2

- Front and off-center to the stage, as well as all the way up to the back of the theater
- Wooden benches that are long and communal
- Least expensive; as low as $1 in the topmost rows

Insider Tips

★ A beloved tradition amongst local Bowl enthusiasts is having a pre-show picnic on the grounds. Picnic tables and choice lawn spots are available on a first-come basis, so it is best to arrive when the gates open, usually 2 hours before showtime.

★ You can bring your own food and beverages, including wine, to savor before and during a show. Alternatively, you can order picnic boxes ($34+), or box seat meals ($26-$100+), via HollywoodBowl.com/foodandwine or (323) 850-1885 before 4pm, the day before your concert. There are also several restaurants on-site as well as an al fresco wine bar.

★ Seniors (age 65+) can get same-day tickets to official Bowl events on select Tuesdays and Thursdays for only $10; call the box office for availability.

★ If you spring for box seats and would like to add a touch of romance, you can bring your own LED candles or purchase approved candles at the Bowl store on-site.

★ If you get bench seat tickets, for added comfort, you can rent seat cushions for $1 at the Bowl or bring your own.

★ Forgo the horrendous traffic to the Bowl by parking for free at one of over a dozen lots in the LA area—i.e., closer to your lodging!—and then taking a shuttle straight to the Bowl. You can view parking locations and purchase shuttle tickets for $7, up to 48 hours in advance, on HollywoodBowl.com; or $12 on-the-day (cash only, exact change required).

★ DO arrive before showtime. If you are late, you may have to wait until intermission to be escorted to your seat.

★ DO bring a jacket and/or blanket. The temperature will most certainly drop once the sun sets.

★ DO bring a bottle of California wine and wine glasses, if so desired (permitted at official Bowl events only).

★ DO NOT bring wine, wine glasses, alcoholic beverages, glass containers or aluminum cans to lease events.

★ DO NOT bring: an oversized picnic basket or cooler larger than 15x15x22 in (38x38x55 cm); a professional recording device; or laser pointer. Flash photography is also prohibited.

★ You can take a self-guided tour of the Bowl and visit its small museum year-round. Hours during the Bowl's official season (June-Sept) are Tue-Sat, 10am-showtime and Sun, 4pm-showtime. During the off-season (Oct-May), opening hours are Tue-Fri, 10am-5pm. Parking is free before 4:30pm.

★ A special way to experience the Bowl, sans the crowds, is by attending one of the LA Phil's morning rehearsals in the Bowl for free... with free parking as well! Rehearsals usually take place Tuesday and Thursday, 9am-noon; and Friday, 10am-noon. Call the box office for confirmed dates.

Notable Nearby

Greek Theatre
(4 mi / 6.5 km away)
Just a short distance from the Bowl is another LA amphitheatre, boasting 6,000 seats and great natural acoustics, where you can rock out with artists like Damien Marley, Culture Club, Los Lonely Boys, Ingrid Michaelson and Thievery Corporation.

Ticket prices vary: LAGreekTheatre.com • Shows held Apr-Sept • Outside food not permitted; you can pre-order food online at least 48 hours before for $15-$20+ • (323) 665-5857 • Parking $15-$30+ • 2700 North Vermont Ave

Ford Amphitheatre
(0.7 mi / 1.1 km away)
Founded in 1920, this intimate amphitheatre (only 1,200 seats), is unique in that it is devoted to showcasing music, dance and theater performances by local arts organizations; and stories that reflect the cultural diversity of LA.

Tickets $12-$100+ via FordTheatres.org • Shows held May-Oct; tickets available in early April • You can bring food and beverages for a pre-show picnic (gates

Rockin' the intensity at The Roxy • Barefoot and mellifluous at the Greek Theatre

open 2 hours before showtime); on-site dining options are also available • (323) 461-3673 • Parking $5-$10 • Metro Rail: Universal City / Studio City (red), plus free shuttle to theatre (evenings only) • 2580 Cahuenga Blvd East

The Roxy
(3 mi / 5 km away)
Spend a night at The Roxy! Since 1973, this legendary music venue has headlined countless indie bands and pop artists; and helped kickstart the careers of The Clash, Sex Pistols, Depeche Mode, Red Hot Chili Peppers, No Doubt, Kings of Leon, et. al.

Tickets via TheRoxy.com • Concerts are generally standing room only • (310) 278-9457 • Valet parking $7-$10+ • 9009 West Sunset Blvd

The Viper Room
(4 mi / 6.5 km away)
Rock out to a metal, punk or alt rock band at this storied club that was once a mobster hangout in the 1930s and where Counting Crows frontman, Adam Duritz, bartended for fun in the '90s, shortly after Johnny Depp acquired the club and christened

it, *The Viper Room*.

Tickets $10-$20+ via ViperRoom.com • Must be age 21+ • (310) 358-1881• Parking $4-$6+ after 6pm at 8755 West Sunset Blvd • 8852 West Sunset Blvd

The Troubadour
(5 mi / 8 km away)

For 60 years, the Troubadour has played host to live concerts featuring up and comers and rock legends alike. And it has enjoyed a long history of surprise concerts by icons like Bob Dylan, Prince, Tom Petty and a reunited Guns N' Roses. Who knows... you might exit this club with your own surprise concert story to tell!

Tickets via Troubadour.com • Concerts are generally standing room only • (310) 276-1158• Parking $6-$9+ at 625 North San Vicente Blvd (garage closes at 2am) • 9081 Santa Monica Blvd

Dining Nearby

Lala's Argentine Grill
(2.8 mi / 4.5 km away)
Argentinian ◆ Empanadas, pasta, sandwiches, seafood, steak
$15-$50+ • Sun-Thu, 11am-11pm; Fri-Sat, 11am-midnight • (323) 934-6838 • 7229 Melrose Ave

Petit Trois
(2.5 mi / 4 km away)
French ◆ Bouillabaisse, salad, soup, carne, seafood, steak
$25-$65+ • noon-11pm • (323) 468-8916 • 718 North Highland Ave

Pizzeria Mozza ★

(2.3 mi / 3.7 km away)

> 'ONE OF LA'S 10 BEST RESTAURANTS' – *LOS ANGELES TIMES*

Italian ◆ Brunch, *pate*, gelato, panini, pizza, salad, carne, seafood
$20-$50+ • ☑ *Reservations* • *noon-midnight* • *(323) 297-0101* • 641 North Highland Ave

Providence ★ ★

(2.5 mi / 4 km away)

> 'LA'S BEST RESTAURANT' 4 YEARS IN A ROW – *LOS ANGELES TIMES*

Seafood ◆ Foie gras, sashimi, duck, lobster, sea urchin, wagyu
$70-$325+ • ☑ *Reservations* • *Mon-Thu, 6pm-10pm; Fri, noon-2pm & 6pm-10pm; Sat, 5:30pm-10pm; Sun, 5:30pm-9pm* • *(323) 460-4170* • 5955 Melrose Ave

Stout

(1.3 mi / 2.1 km away)
American ◆ Burgers, cole slaw, fries, onion rings, veggie burgers
$20-$30+ • *11:30am-4am* • *(323) 469-3801* • 1544 North Cahuenga Blvd

Tender Greens

(1.5 mi / 2.5 km away)
American ◆ Falafel, salad, sandwiches, soup, carne, seafood, steak
$15-$20+ • *11:00am-10:00pm* • *(323) 382-0380* • 6290 Sunset Blvd

Hollywood Sign

For nearly a century, the Hollywood Sign has served as a beacon of inspiration for generations of dreamers and achievers, including the movie stars of today and yesteryear, who are as iconic as the Sign itself.

2 Fantastic Ways to Gaze Upon the Sign

Goeth on Foot... for a View to Remember

There are a number of hiking trails that will take you to the rear of the Hollywood Sign. You should know, however, that you will not be able to get within arms length as the Sign is fenced in, guarded and under constant surveillance.

Yet, you may find that the views of LA along the way are well worth the climb.

Via the Wonder View Trail, you can hike 3 miles (4.8 km) roundtrip to the rear of the Sign. The trail is rough in places and boasts a

850-foot (259 m) elevation gain.

Be sure to bring bottled water and refrain from hiking in the heat of mid-day. And, if you can, go on a super clear and sunny day, when views along the way will be at their most stellar.

> *Drive to Lake Hollywood Dr & Wonder View Dr. Park on Lake Hollywood Dr (permissible 5am-7pm); then walk east on Wonder View Dr to the trailhead*

Goeth by Car... for a Great Photo Op

The Hollywood Sign is perched atop Mount Lee in the Hollywood Hills. It is not directly accessible by car, as the only road leading up to the sign is open to authorized personnel only.

However, you can easily drive to Lake Hollywood Park, a dog park situated directly beneath the Sign. This is the best place to get a close and unobstructed photo with the Sign—no hiking required!

> *5am–10:30pm • Picnic tables, barbecue pits • (323) 913-4688 • 3160 Canyon Lake Dr*

Notable Nearby

Cinespia at Hollywood Forever Cemetery
(3 mi / 5 km away)
Visit the graves of film legends Rudolph Valentino, Jayne Mansfield,

Stellar views abound atop the Griffith Park Observatory

Mickey Rooney, Cecil B. DeMille, Tyrone Power, et. al. Then settle in for an outdoor screening of an iconic movie in this star-studded cemetery, with live DJs and elaborate photo booths to boot!

Cinespia screenings: $15; 7pm on weekends (May-Oct). For showtimes and tickets: Cinespia.org • Cemetery visiting hours: Mon-Fri, 8:30am-5pm; Sat-Sun, 8:30am-4:30pm • (323) 469-1181 • 6000 Santa Monica Blvd

Griffith Park Observatory
(5.5 mi / 9 km away)
One of the few places in the world where you can gaze, for free, at sunspots and solar flares through high-powered solar telescopes; and at planets, comets and stars through night refractor telescopes. It is also a great place to take in sweeping views of the City of Angels below.

Free! • Noon-10pm, generally; closed Mon • (213) 473-0800 • Metro Rail: Vermont / Sunset station (red), then take the DASH shuttle ($1 roundtrip) to the Observatory • Parking $4 an hour • 2800 East Observatory Rd

Lake Hollywood Loop Trail

(2.5 mi / 4 km away)

Enjoy a jog or stroll along this easy, 3.4 mile (5.5 km) trail that loops around a city reservoir of turquoise water reflecting the Hollywood Sign nearby. On the southern end of the reservoir, you can stand on a bridge for a nice photo op with the Sign.

Gates to the trailhead are open 6:30am-6pm, generally (closes as late as 7:30pm, May-Aug) • Dogs are not permitted on the trail • Limited off-street parking available at the Weidlake gate: 6397 Weidlake Dr

Mulholland Drive

(4 mi / 6.5 km away)

This topsy-curvy mountain road, which stretches 11 miles (18 km) through the Hollywood Hills, has inspired many a struggling actor, from Naomi Watts to Jim Carrey. Why? Because it offers stunning views of LA, the city where dreams can come true.

Start: 6701 Mulholland Dr • End: 15653 Mulholland Dr • Or vice versa!

Echo Park Lake

(5.4 mi / 8.6 km away)

A relaxing oasis in the heart of Los Angeles where you can take in great views of Downtown LA whilst picnicking by, strolling along or pedal boating around a lovely lake brimming with fish, turtles, waterfowl and lotus flowers.

Pedal boat $10 (1 hr); guided canoe ride $10 (25 min, Sat-Sun); guided gondola ride $50-$75 per couple (30 min, Sat-Sun). Cash only. Rental hours: 9am-sunset • Food concessions available 9am-3pm at the boathouse • (213) 481-8577 • 751 North Echo Park Ave

Big Bear Lake

(100 mi | 161 km away)

When Los Angelenos want to escape the heat in summer or catch some powder in winter, they head up to Big Bear, a beautiful, snow-fed lake surrounded by mountains and forests of pine—ripe for boating, parasailing, fishing, hiking, biking, et. al., in summer; and skiing, snowboarding, tubing, et. al., in winter.

Big Bear's ski slopes are nowhere as splendid as ones in Northern California, but they are an okay alternative and only a 2 hour drive from LA • Snow tires or chains are required when driving here in winter • Visitors Center: (909) 866-7000 • 630 Bartlett Rd, Big Bear

Dining Nearby

Birds Cafe-Bar

(2.5 mi | 4 km away)
American ◆ Rotisserie chicken, salad, burgers, tacos, sandwiches
$15-$20+ • 11am-11pm • (323) 465-0175 • 5925 Franklin Ave

Bourgeois Pig

(2.5 mi | 4 km away)
American ◆ Coffee, tea, muffins, quiche, soup, salad, sandwiches
$5-$15+ • 8am-2am • (323) 464-6008 • 5931 Franklin Ave

Cleo

(2.5 mi | 4.5 km away)
Mediterranean, Tapas ◆ Flatbreads, pasta, carne, seafood, steak

$20-$40+ • ☑ Reservations • Sun-Wed, 6pm-10pm; Thu-Sat, 6pm-11pm • (323) 962-1711 • 1717 Vine St

Ruen Pair
(3.5 mi / 5.5 km away)
Thai ◆ Curry, noodles, mussels, soup, salad, carne, duck, seafood
$10+ • 11am-3am • (323) 466-0153 • 5257 Hollywood Blvd

Shintaro
(4 mi / 6 km away)
Japanese ◆ Sushi, noodles, edamame, teriyaki, soup, salad
$10-$30+ • ☑ Reservations • 11:30am-2:30am • (323) 882-6524 • 1900 North Highland Ave

The Trails Cafe
(3.5 mi / 5.5 km away)
Vegetarian ◆ Coffee, tea, quiche, muffins, sandwiches
$5-$20+ • 8am-5pm • (323) 871-2102 • 2333 Fern Dell Dr

Fall under the spell of the Magic Castle, where members of the Academy of Magical Arts and the world's greatest magicians gather nightly to enthrall and delight with tricks n' illusions, old and new.

*Enter a World of Magic...
By Invitation Only*

The Magic Castle is a private club with members ranging from big-name magicians like Penn & Teller, Lance Burton and David Blaine... to Hollywood stars like Zoe Saldana, Nicolas Cage, Steve Martin, Chrissy Teigen and Neil Patrick Harris.

Unless you know a member or get a coveted chance to become one (for $2,000+, plus a few sleights of hand), there are only two ways to gain a special guest pass into its hallowed walls:

Stay at the Magic Castle Hotel

The Magic Castle Hotel is perched right in the heart of Hollywood, just steps from the Castle itself. Room rates are $190-$350+, which is a pretty good deal given that you are just 2 blocks away from the action on Hollywood Boulevard.

When you book a room reservation at the Magic Castle Hotel, you should indicate at the time of your booking that you are interested in visiting the Magic Castle during your stay. This is most easily done via phone, (323) 851-0800, but you can also email reservations@magiccastlehotel.com.

The hotel will check availability and make a dining reservation at the Castle on your behalf (all guests to the Castle are required to partake of dinner or brunch during their visit).

Become a Member of S.A.M or I.B.M

Members of the Society of American Magicians and the International Brotherhood of Magicians are granted an honorary guest pass to the Castle.

To become a member of either society, you can apply online via MagicSam.com or Magician.org. Annual dues are $65-$85 for S.A.M. and $75-$105 for I.B.M.

All guests to the Castle are required to partake of dinner or brunch during their visit, and dining reservations must be made in advance.

To make a dining reservation, simply call (323) 851-3313; indicate that you are a S.A.M. or I.B.M member; check to see if your desired date is available; then reserve your spot with a credit card.

Planning Guide

The Magic Castle is open year-round and dining reservations can be made for an evening visit any day of the week (must be age 21+); or a brunch visit on weekends only (no age limit). Your reservation can be for up to 6 people.

You CANNOT enter the Castle without an advanced dining reservation, by way of a guest pass.

More Info	MagicCastle.com	(323) 851-3313
Price	$20 cover on Mon-Thu evenings & Sat-Sun brunch; $30 cover, Fri-Sun evenings. (The cover is waived for you and 1 guest if you are a S.A.M. or I.B.M member residing outside of California). Additionally, brunch or dinner service is required and is $30-$50+ for adults; $20+ for ages 10 and under.
Hours	Mon–Fri, 5pm-2am; Sat-Sun, 10am-3pm & 5pm-2am
Policies	Smoking is prohibited. For evening visits, all guests must show a valid, government-issued ID. Dining reservations can be canceled or changed up to 24 hours before. If one or more in your party is a no-show, you will be charged $25 per person.
Parking	$13, valet only
Metro Rail	Hollywood & Highland (red), plus 3 block walk
Map It	7001 Franklin Ave

Insider Tips

★ The best time to visit is on a Friday or Saturday evening when there are usually more magicians and performances in the Castle and all of the public rooms are open, making for a more magical experience.

★ You can view the week's lineup of magicians on the Castle's website. Schedules are posted a month in advance.

★ A special time to visit the Castle is during the last week of October, when it celebrates its biggest holiday—Halloween. During Halloween week, the Castle is ghoulishly decorated and attendees come decked out in their favorite costumes.

★ I highly suggest arriving before doors to the Castle open. That way, you can be one of the first in line for the Close-Up Gallery, located in the hallway to your left once you enter the first floor of the Castle. The Gallery fills up quickly and can be harder to get into as the evening progresses.

★ The Magic Castle has a very strict dress code policy (posted on its website) and you could be turned away if it is not followed. For evening events, the dress code is evening attire; and for weekend brunch, casual chic.

★ When the spotlights are on above the piano in Irma's Room on the first floor, the Castle's most musical ghost is open for special requests. Ask Irma to play one of your favorite songs and, when she does, show your appreciation by ordering her

Just jokin' around at The Comedy Store and Laugh Factory

a drink from the bar or a roving cocktail waiter. Then wait to see what happens next!

★ As a Magic Castle Hotel guest, you can ride a free shuttle up and down the steep driveway to the Castle's entrance, which is especially convenient if you are wearing high heels.

Notable Nearby

Laugh Factory
(1.7 mi / 2.7 km away)
Since Richard Pryor headlined its opening night in 1979, this comedy club has been an LA haven for comedians like Jim Carrey, Chris Rock, Ellen DeGeneres and Jamie Foxx. And it is notorious for its celebrity drop-ins—when *kahunas* like Kevin Hart and Adam Sandler drop by unannounced to do an impromptu set.

Tickets $10-$40+ via LaughFactory.com; 2 drink minimum (during show); must *be age 18+ • Showtimes 8pm, 10pm & midnight, generally • (323) 656-1336 • Valet parking $7 • 8001 Sunset Blvd*

The Comedy Store

(2.3 mi / 3.7 km away)

Get your laugh on at this old school Hollywood club where actor Pauly Shore grew up watching Whoopi Goldberg, Jay Leno and Robin Williams before they were household names. Shore's parents founded the club in 1972; and he manages it today.

Tickets $10-$20 via TheComedyStore.com; 2 drink minimum; must be age 21+ • 7pm-2am, showtimes vary • (323) 650-6268 • 8433 Sunset Blvd

The Groundlings

(1.1 mi / 1.8 km away)

Try not to split your funny bone at this improv and sketch comedy theatre where Melissa McCarthy, Lisa Kudrow, Kathy Griffin, Kristen Wiig and Will Ferrell got their start. Its signature show, *Cookin' With Gas*, on Thursday nights, oft has a celebrity guest on stage hamming it up with the main cast.

Tickets $18 via Groundlings.com; must be age 16+ • Showtimes 8pm & 10pm, generally • No late seating, arrive early • (323) 934-4747 • Valet parking $7 on Melrose Ave & North Poinsettia Place • 7307 Melrose Ave

El Rey Theatre

(3.5 mi / 5.5 km away)

Catch a live concert with an indie band or pop star like Justin Timberlake, Leann Rhimes or Cage the Elephant at this lovely Art Deco theatre that was erected as a movie palace in 1936.

Tickets and showtimes via TheElRey.com • Concerts standing room only, generally • Full bar and food service on-site • (323) 936-6400 • 5515 Wilshire Blvd

Venice Boardwalk

The Venice Boardwalk is delightfully unique; a place where people can truly be whoever or whatever they want, no matter how zany or weird. And that freedom of self-expression is always on display in a big way on this historic boardwalk by the sea.

Planning Guide

The Venice Boardwalk is an awesome place for people watching... from sun-kissed surfers to sun-tanned weightlifters to a smorgasboard of street performers who really know how to put on a show.

The Boardwalk spans 1 mile (1.5 km), from Muscle Beach in the south to the city of Santa Monica in the north. It is lined with shops and street vendors selling zany t-shirts and souvenirs, as well as whimsical art and handmade crafts by local artists.

A stone's throw from the Boardwalk is a lovely sandy beach that stretches on for 3 miles (5 km) and is popular with surfers who live nearby. There is also a skateboard park and a wide bike path that meanders 6 miles (9 km) through Venice and Santa Monica.

Amenities	Lifeguards on duty 9am-sunset; restrooms; showers; handball, basketball and volleyball courts; fishing pier
Policies	No walking on bike path; no cyclists, roller skaters, etc., on the Boardwalk. No smoking on the beach or in the park. No dogs on the Boardwalk, June-Oct.
Parking	$9+ in lot at 1900 Ocean Front Walk
Metro Rail + Bus	4th & Colorado (Expo line); walk 2 blocks to Broadway & 3rd; catch the Santa Monica 1 bus to Windward & Main; walk 1 block to the Boardwalk
Map It	1800 Ocean Front Walk

Insider Tips

★ If you want to experience the full Venice Boardwalk vibe, the best time to go is on a weekend afternoon. This will also be the most crowded time to go.

★ Alternatively, you can go on a weekday after noon (12pm). Though you will see fewer street performers, you can still interact with local artists, artisans and other vendors minus the crush and musk of hundreds of tourists.

★ Bring $1 and $5 bills to tip the street performers you enjoy.

★ You can rent bikes, skateboards and roller skates at shops near the bike path for as low as $6 an hour or $20 for the day. You can also rent beach chairs and umbrellas, surfboards, boogie boards, paddleboards and wetsuits.

★ Get a bird's eye view of the Boardwalk atop High Rooftop Lounge. The food is mediocre, but the views during sunset more than make up for it. ($10-$40+; Mon-Thu, 3pm-10pm (happy hour 7pm-9:30pm), Fri, 3pm-midnight; Sat, noon-midnight; Sun, noon-10pm; 1697 Pacific Ave)

★ Want to work out at the infamous Muscle Beach? You can purchase a day pass to the gym for $10; open 8am-7pm (Apr-Sept), closes earlier Oct-Mar; (310) 399-2775.

★ Parking lots fill up quickly on summer weekends (June-early Sept); I highly suggest arriving before 10am.

Clockwise: Skateboarder cruisin' down the Boardwalk • Sailing out of Marina del Rey Harbor • A gorgeous day in the Venice Canal Historic District

★ Venice Beach does experience rip currents—very strong waves close to shore that can carry you out to sea. If you get caught in one, swim parallel to the ocean until you are out of the current. Before getting in the ocean, ask a lifeguard if there are any rip currents nearby.

★ DO NOT swim or surf in the ocean 3 to 5 days after a rainstorm as there is likely to be debris and bacteria, washed in from nearby storm drains, that could cause injury or illness.

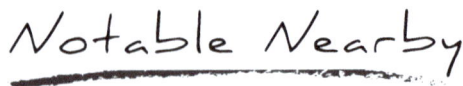

South Bay Coastal Trail
(South end: 13.5 mi | 21.5 km away)
LA's South Bay is home to the tony seaside communities of Manhattan Beach, Hermosa Beach and Redondo Beach, which share a scenic walking and biking trail that coasts for 6 miles, taking you past surfers, volleyballers, piers and million dollar homes.

Bike rental $9+/hour, $27+/day at Marina Bike Rentals where you can park free with bike rental (Mon-Fri, 10am-sunset; Sat-Sun, 9am-sunset; (310) 318-2453; 505 North Harbor Dr, Redondo Beach). From there, bike north to Manhattan Beach and back! Trail map: TheYOLOGuide.com/california/braude-map

Marina del Rey Harbor
(2.5 mi | 4 km away)
Embark on a kayaking, paddleboarding, sailing, jet skiing or parasailing adventure amidst sea lions and herons in the Marina del Rey harbor... and beyond into the Pacific Ocean.

VisitMarinadelRey.com/things-to-do/on-the-water

Santa Monica Pier
(2.5 mi | 4 km away)
On this historic pier, built in 1909, you can ride a nearly 100-year-old wooden carousel; take trapeze lessons; and enjoy a sunset by the beach while perched 130 ft (40 m) above the ocean on the world's first solar-powered Ferris wheel.

Carousel $2; LA Trapeze School $35-$87; Pacific Wheel $8 • Attraction hours vary • Parking $2-$15 • Metro Rail: Downtown Santa Monica (Expo line), plus 5 block walk • 200 Santa Monica Pier, Santa Monica

Third Street Promenade
(2.5 mi | 4 km away)
An open-air marketplace with shops and restaurants; boasts a fun mix of street musicians and performers, especially on weekends.

Public parking $1-$14; first 90 minutes free • Metro Rail: Downtown Santa Monica (Expo line), plus 2 block walk • 3rd Street & Broadway, Santa Monica

Abbot Kinney Boulevard
(0.6 mi | 1 km away)
Abbot Kinney Boulevard is at the epicenter of an historic and bohemian artist enclave that is now home to eclectic shops, art galleries, bars and restaurants fit for a foodie.

1300 Abbot Kinney Blvd

Venice Canal Historic District
(0.5 mi | 750 m away)
Stroll along the last remaining canals of the *Venice of California*, a network of 6 canals and 9 footbridges, flanked by low-key million dollar homes, colorful gardens and private docks.

2201 Dell Ave

Dining Nearby

26 Beach
(1.5 mi | 2.5 km away)
American ◆ Breakfast, salad, pasta, burgers, carne, seafood, steak

$20-$30+ • ☑ Reservations • Mon-Thu, 8am-9:30pm; Fri-Sat, 8am-10pm; Sun, 8am-9pm • (310) 823-7526 • 3100 West Washington Blvd, Marina del Rey

Abbot's Pizza Co.

(0.7 mi l 1 km away)
Italian ◆ Gourmet pizza, New York-style pizza, salad, calzones
$20-$30+ • Sun-Thu, 11am-11pm; Fri-Sat, 11am-midnight • (310) 396-7334
• 1407 Abbot Kinney Blvd, Venice

Flake

(1 mi l 2 km away)
American ◆ Breakfast, salad, panini, wraps
$10+ • 7am-3:30pm • (310) 396-2333 • 513 Rose Ave, Venice

Gjelina

(0.7 mi l 1.2 km away)
American ◆ Breakfast, salad, pizza, oysters, carne, seafood, steak
$30-$50+ • ☑ Reservations • 8am-midnight • (310) 450-1429 • 1429 Abbot Kinney Blvd, Venice

Poke-Poke

(0.1 mi l 160 m away)
Hawaiian ◆ Poke bowls, acai bowls
$10-$20+ • 11am-6pm • (310) 822-5639 • 2011 Ocean Front Walk, Venice

Rustic Canyon Wine Bar and Seasonal Kitchen

(3.6 mi l 5.8 km away)
American ◆ Mussels, ricotta, salad, carne, seafood, steak
$55-$80+ • ☑ Reservations • Sun-Thu, 5:30pm-10:30pm; Fri-Sat, 5:30pm-11pm • (310) 393-7050 • 1119 Wilshire Blvd, Santa Monica

The J. Paul Getty Museum is the world's wealthiest museum and it boasts 2 locations — the Getty Center and Getty Villa — both of which are a harmony of world-class art and architecture, home to masterpieces from antiquity to today.

Planning Guide

Getty Center

The Getty Center is perched atop a mount in West LA, with fantastic views of the city below.

It is comprised of five pavilions filled with art from medieval times to present day—paintings, sculptures, drawings, decorative arts, illuminated manuscripts and photography.

And it is home to a bevy of heavy hitters—Van Gogh's *Irises* (1889) alongside European masterpieces by Cezanne, da Vinci, Degas, Gauguin, Goya, Manet, Michelangelo, Monet, Pissarro, Raphael, Rembrandt and Renoir... just to name a few!

More Info	Getty.edu/visit/center	(310) 440-7300
Admission	Free!
Hours	Tue–Fri & Sun, 10am-5:30pm; Sat 10am-9pm
Tours	Free guided tours of the art, gardens and architecture are offered daily at select times, which are posted online
Parking	$15 ($10 after 3pm)
Metro Rail + Bus	Expo / Sepulveda (Expo line), then catch the 734 bus (Mon-Fri) or 234 (Sat-Sun) bus to the Center
Map It	North Sepulveda Blvd & Getty Center Dr

Getty Villa

The Getty Villa is nestled on a hill near Malibu, with lovely views of the Pacific Ocean. Its architecture and gardens are modeled after the Villa dei Papyri, which was built during the Roman Empire.

Within its classical walls is a magnificent array of 1,200 statues, frescoes and ancient artifacts from its permanent collection of 44,000 works of art spanning 7,000 years of antiquity.

Out of doors, the Villa's gardens are also a main attraction, for they contain 300+ plant varieties, including herbs, flowers and fruit trees that were grown in the villas of ancient Rome.

More Info	Getty.edu/visit/villa	(310) 440-7300
Admission	Free! But reservations must be made online in advance
Hours	Tue–Fri & Sun, 10am-5:30pm; Sat 10am-9pm

Clockwise: Overlooking Surfrider Beach from Malibu Pier • 'Standing Woman' (1932) by Gaston Lachaise, in the Franklin D. Murphy Sculpture Garden • A tranquil courtyard at the Getty Villa

Tours	Free guided tours of the art, gardens and architecture are offered daily at select times, which are posted online
Parking	$15 ($10 after 3pm)
Metro Rail + Bus	Downtown Santa Monica (Expo line), then walk 1 block to 5th St & Colorado Ave and catch the 534 bus to the Villa. Make sure the driver hole-punches your printed ticket to the Villa; you will not be able to walk through the Villa's gates without proof you arrived by bus.
Map It	17985 Pacific Coast Hwy

Insider Tips

★ For fantastic views of Los Angeles, visit the Getty Center's Cactus Garden, located behind the South and West Pavilions.

★ At the Getty Center, you can enjoy a picnic on the lawn overlooking the Central Garden. You are welcome to bring your own food. Or you can order picnic boxes online in advance; or purchase lunch and snacks at one of the cafes on-site.

★ If you are in the mood for a more upscale dining experience, reserve a table with a view at The Restaurant at the Getty Center ($25-$110+; Tue-Fri, 11:30am-2:30pm; Sat, 11:30 am-2:30pm & 5pm-9pm; Sun, 11am-3pm; (310) 440-6810).

★ From the Getty Center parking lot, you can ride a free tram to the museum's entrance; or you can take a more scenic, 15-minute walk up a moderately steep hill via a paved path that offers great vistas of the museum and surrounds.

★ The Getty Villa has an outdoor terrace where you can order a bottle of wine and a cheese plate or Mediterranean platter from the Villa Cafe and treat yourself to classical views and cool breezes from the Pacific Ocean nearby.

★ If you plan to visit the Villa and the Center on the same day, you can park at both locations for the price of one. Simply visit the Information Desk at either location to obtain a voucher for same-day complimentary parking at the other.

★ Both the Villa and the Center offer monthly culinary workshops inspired by a period in art history. During the workshop, you will be taken on a gallery tour to view artwork from that period and then to pick herbs in the garden (for Villa workshops only), after which you will get to prepare a meal based on recipes found in ancient diaries and the like ($85, includes parking; reservations: Getty.edu/visit/cal/food.html).

★ Both the Center and the Villa host concerts and theatrical performances on select dates year-round: Getty.edu/visit/cal/performances.html; many of them for the cost of free.

Notable Nearby

Bergamot Station Art Galleries
(7 mi / 11 km from Getty Center and Getty Villa)
Immerse yourself in a world of contemporary art at this railroad station turned art gallery complex that is home to nearly 40 galleries, many of which feature works by local artists.

Tue-Fri, 10am-6pm; Sat, 11am-5:30pm • Artist talks and receptions held regularly: BergamotStation.com • Cafe on-site, serving soup, salad, sandwiches, et. al. (Tue-Fri, 9am-5pm; Sat, 10am-5pm) • (310) 453-7535 • Metro Rail: 26th St / Bergamot (Expo line) • 2525 Michigan Ave, Santa Monica

Franklin D. Murphy Sculpture Garden
(4 mi / 6.2 km from Getty Center)
Treat yourself to a visual feast of over 70 sculptures by venerable artists like Auguste Rodin at this public garden in the heart of the

University of California, Los Angeles (UCLA) campus.

Interactive map: Hammer.ucla.edu/collections • $1-$20 in Parking Structure 3: 215 Charles E. Young Dr • (310) 443-7000 • 245 Charles E. Young Dr

Virginia Robinson Estate & Gardens
(5.5 mi I 9 km from Getty Center)
Spend a sensory afternoon at one of the first luxury homes of Beverly Hills. Built in 1911, the Robinson Estate boasts one of the loveliest private gardens in LA, especially in springtime (Mar-May).

Tours $11, email visit@robinsongardens.org and you will receive an auto-reply with dates of upcoming tours; then reply to RSVP for a desired date and await a confirmation email • (310) 550-2087 • 1008 Elden Way, Beverly Hills

Surfrider Beach, Malibu
(6.5 mi I 10 km from Getty Villa)
As the first inductee into the World Surfing Reserve due to its "stellar waves," this Malibu beach is blessed with super long breaks that make for *bodacious* riding for surfing enthusiasts; and fun surfer-spectating for those watching from ashore.

Lifeguards on duty 9am-sunset, generally • Food concessions, restrooms, showers, beach volleyball courts and a fishing pier • $30 to rent a surfboard and wetsuit for 24 hours from Zuma Jay's (located across the street from the pier) • Parking $3-$14 • 23050 Pacific Coast Hwy, Malibu

Point Mugu Sand Dune & Ray Miller Trail
(28 mi I 45 km from Getty Villa)
Go sledding or *sole surfing* down a 400-foot (122 m) sand dune atop of which you may spy whales and dolphins at play in the seas below. Then embark on a 5.4 mile I 8.7 km (roundtrip), moderate hike in the Santa Monica Mountains via the Ray Miller Trail, which is on the north end of the newly completed Backbone Trail (67

mi | 108 km long), one of the longest trails in SoCal. During your hike, you will be treated to lovely panoramas of rugged canyons and chaparral to the east; and endless ocean waves to the west.

The dune is located on the side of the highway, just south of Thornhill Broome Beach & Campground: 9000 West Pacific Coast Hwy, Malibu. The road to the Ray Miller Trailhead parking lot (open 8am-sunset) is just north of Broome Beach (look for a sign reading La Jolla Canyon) • Day use beach parking $8 • Tent / RV camping $35 on the beach; $10 in Sycamore Canyon Campground nearby. Campsites reservable 7 months in advance via ReserveAmerica.com. • Via CampingAdventuresRentals.com, you can rent an RV and have it delivered to the campground prior to your arrival ($187-$262+; 2-night minimum).

Dining Nearby

Getty Center

Palomino
(3.3 mi | 5.3 km away)
Mediterranean ♦ Salad, soup, pasta, pizza, carne, seafood, steak
$20-$60+ • Mon-Sat, 11am-10pm; Sun, 11am-9pm • (310) 208-1960 • 10877 Wilshire Blvd, Suite 150

Plan Check Kitchen + Bar
(3.8 mi | 6.2 km away)
American ♦ Breakfast, salad, burgers, cheesesteaks, panini
$20-$30+ • Sun-Wed, 11:30am-10pm; Thu, 11:30am-11pm; Fri-Sat, 11:30am-midnight • (310) 444-1411 • 1800 Sawtelle Blvd

Sushi Sasabune
(3.6 mi / 5.7 km away)
Japanese ✦ Sushi, sashimi
$20+ • ☑ Reservations • Mon-Fri, noon-2pm & 5:30pm-10pm; Sat, 5:30pm-10pm • (310) 478-3596 • 11917 Wilshire Blvd

Getty Villa

Grom Malibu
(8.5 mi / 14 km away)
Gelato ✦ Gelato, fruit sorbet, hot cocoa, milkshakes
$5+ • Mon-Thu, noon-9pm; Fri, noon-10pm; Sat, 11am-10pm; Sun, 11am-9pm • (310) 456-9797 • 3888 Cross Creek Rd, Malibu

Malibu Seafood
(12.5 mi / 20 km away)
Seafood ✦ Clam chowder, fish n' chips, salad, sandwiches, seafood
$15-$35+ • 11am-7:30pm • (310) 456-3430 • 25653 Pacific Coast Hwy, Malibu

Moonshadows Malibu
(4.5 mi / 7.5 km away)
American ✦ Pasta, salad, sandwiches, carne, seafood, steak
$25-$80+ • ☑ Reservations • 11:30am-10pm, generally • (310) 456-3010 • 20356 Pacific Coast Hwy, Malibu

Gaze in awe upon the well-preserved skeletons of saber-toothed cats, mammoths, dire wolves and other seemingly fantastical beasts that roamed the hills and valleys of Los Angeles 40,000 years ago.

Planning Guide

La Brea Tar Pits is one of the largest deposits of Ice Age fossils in the world. Since the early 1900s, more than 3 million specimens have been excavated here, some of which you can view up close at the Page Museum nearby.

The museum takes less than a hour to peruse, but if you have never seen a well-preserved skeleton of a saber-toothed cat, 6-foot sloth or Columbian mammoth, you are in for a treat.

Out of doors, you can stroll past tar pits large and small, which are viewable at any time for free. Despite the name, the pits are not comprised of tar, but rather asphalt, the lowest grade of petroleum and a natural substance. (Tar is man-made.)

More Info	TarPits.org	(213) 763-3499
Admission	$12
Hours	9:30am-5pm
Tour	The 1-hr Excavator Tour will take you to a partially excavated pit filled with prehistoric bones. Tour meets by the museum's Fossil Lab: Mon-Fri, 1pm & 2:30pm; Sat-Sun, noon & 2pm. Reservations are free, first-come and can fill up on weekends, so come early.
Metro Rail + Bus	Wilshire / Western (purple), then take the 20 bus to Wilshire St & Curson Ave
Parking	$10, on the corner of Curson Ave & 6th St
Map It	5801 Wilshire Blvd

Notable Nearby

Los Angeles County Museum of Art
(0.4 mi / 600 m away)
For a county museum, LACMA is first-rate. It is the largest art museum on the West Coast, with an impressive collection of art from antiquity to today, like *Metropolis II* (2011), a sculpted city with 1,100 mini cars traveling 240 scale mph (386 kph).

Admission $15; free second Tue of month • Mon-Tue & Thu, 11am-5pm; Fri, 11am-8pm; Sat-Sun, 10am-7pm • Metropolis II runs at select times, Fri-Sun • Free guided tours offered daily, times posted online. • Free outdoor concerts Fri-Sun (Apr-Nov); free concerts in the Bing Theatre every Sunday: LACMA.org/events-calendar. • Parking $14 • (323) 857-6010 • 5905 Wilshire Blvd

Petersen Automotive Museum
(0.4 mi / 600 m away)
So much of California has been shaped by one of the greatest inventions of modern times—the automobile. At the Petersen, you can view 100 years' worth of innovation in the form of 300 cars and motorcycles, including a 1936 Bugatti worth $40 million.

Admission $15 • 10am-6pm • 1-Hour Vault Tour: $20; times vary; reservable via Petersen.org • (323) 930-2277 • Parking $12 • 6060 Wilshire Blvd

Rodeo Drive & The Golden Triangle
(3 mi / 4.8 km away)
Shop or window shop to your heart's content in this posh fashion mecca, home to over 100 high-end and mid-range boutiques, including American fashion houses like Tory Burch and Tom Ford.

The Triangle's borders are Santa Monica Blvd, Wilshire Blvd & Canon Dr • Store directory: LoveBeverlyHills.com • Free 2-hour parking: 9480 Dayton Way

Clockwise: 'Angel's Flight' (1931) by California artist, Millard Sheets, depicts a tenement in Downtown LA in the 1930s; on display at LACMA • 1913 Mercer Raceabout, an American-made sports car, at the Petersen • 'Urban Light' (2008) by American artist Chris Burden, at LACMA

Dining Nearby

Original Farmers Market
(1 mi / 1.6 km away)

Founded in 1934, this is the site of LA's first farmers market, where local farmers sold produce from the back of their trucks. Today, it is a food bazaar with 70+ restaurants and specialty shops serving up an array of international cuisine.

Mon-Fri, 9am-9pm; Sat, 9am-8pm; Sun, 10am-7pm • Bring cash; some vendors do not accept credit cards • Free concerts: Fri, 7pm-9pm (June-Aug) • (323) 933-9211 • Free 90-minute parking with vendor validation • 6333 West 3rd St

Animal

(1.5 mi | 2.4 km away)
American ◆ Brunch, veal, uni, sandwiches, carne, seafood, steak
$20-$70+ • ☑ Reservations • Mon-Fri, 6pm-close; Sat-Sun, 10am-2pm & 6pm-close • (323) 782-9225 • 435 North Fairfax Ave

Blu Jam Cafe

(2.1 mi | 3.4 km away)
American ◆ Breakfast, burgers, salad, sandwiches, seafood, steak
$20-$30+ • 8am-4pm • (323) 951-9191 • 7371 Melrose Ave

Boa Steakhouse

(3.5 mi | 5.5 km away)
Steakhouse ◆ Foie gras, salad, sandwiches, carne, seafood, steak
$20-$140+ • ☑ Reservations • Mon-Fri, 11:30am-2pm & 5:30-until; Sat, 5:30pm-midnight; Sun, 5:30pm-10pm • (310) 278-2050 • 9200 Sunset Blvd

Genwa Korean BBQ

(1.1 mi | 1.8 km away)
Korean ◆ Bimimbap, noodles, soup, carne, seafood, steak
$20-$50+ • ☑ Reservations • Mon-Fri, 11am-10pm; Sat-Sun, noon-10pm • (323) 549-0760 • 5115 Wilshire Blvd

Lucques

(2.3 mi | 3.7 km away)
American ◆ Burger, gnocchi, salad, soup, carne, seafood, steak
$25-$80+ • ☑ Reservations • Mon, 6pm-9:30pm; Tue-Sat, noon-2:30pm & 6pm-close; Sun, 5pm-9:30pm • (323) 655-6277 • 8474 Melrose Ave

In 1932, David Alfaro Siequeiros debuted the world's first spray-painted mural in Downtown LA and the city has never been the same since. Today, LA is so chockful of murals, created by renowned artists from near and afar, you will spot at least one during your time in the Mural Capital of the World.

2 Ways to Mural Art Walk in LA

Join a Guided Tour of the LA Arts District

The LA Arts District has been an enclave for artists and creatives since the 1960s when they began to convert and set up residence in defunct industrial buildings along the west bank of the LA River.

Out of doors, the District's artful influence is on display in a big way on dozens of exteriors that showcase the talent of muralists and street artists from near and afar.

During a 2.5 hour walking tour, with a local muralist as your guide, you will see 50+ murals spanning 30 years, by artists including LA-based muralists El Mac and Shepard Fairey.

Venice Kinesis (2011) by California muralist, Rip Cronk; at 23 Windward Ave near the Venice Boardwalk (p 57) • Previous pages: Untitled (2013) by LA muralist David Choe, and Aryz; near Mateo St & 7th St in DTLA. Redemption of Angels (2013) by LA muralist, Christina Angelina, and Fin DAC; the mural has a new look, which you check out on East 4th St & Merrick St in DTLA

> *Tours $12 via LAArtTours.com/graffititour • Dates vary; generally Thu, Sat & Sun at 11:30am, 1pm and/or 2pm • Be sure to bring bottled water so you can stay hydrated • (310) 503-2365 • Metro Rail: Little Tokyo/ Arts District (gold), plus 7 block walk • Tour meets at 533 Colyton St*

Design a Self-Guided Tour

The best way to see a cadre of murals most pleasing to your artistic palate is to map out your own self-guided tour.

Via MuralConservancy.org/murals, you can search for murals located in and around the neighborhoods where you will be lodging and sightseeing. The greatest concentration of murals can be found in Venice Beach, Hollywood and Downtown LA.

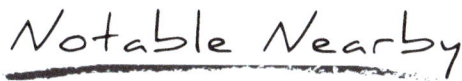

Urban Kayaking on the LA River

(4.8 mi / 7.7 km from LA Arts District)

Discover a different side of LA during a bike + kayak tour of the LA River, which was paved in the 1930s but is slowly being restored to its natural glory as a habitat for fish and waterfowl.

Guided tour $75, reservable via LARiverKayakSafari.org • Tours held on weekends and select weekdays, June-Sept • (213) 308-5390 • Meet at Oso Park: Riverside Dr & Oros St

Watts Tower

(8.3 mi / 13.2 km from LA Arts District)

On a quiet residential street in East LA stands *Nuestro Pueblo* (1955), the Gaudi-esque life's work of Simon Rodia, who worked construction by day and, for 34 years, sculpted sky-high steel and ceramic spires upwards of 99 ft (30 m) in his yard by night.

Guided Tour: $7 • Tours begin every 30 min: Thu-Sat, 10:30am-3pm; Sun, 12:30pm-3pm • (213) 847-4646 • 1727 East 107th St

Norton Simon Museum & Gamble House

(11 mi / 17.5 km from LA Arts District)

Though small in size, Norton Simon is home to an enviable number of heavy hitters: Van Gogh, Rodin, Picasso, Degas, Hiroshige, et. al. A few blocks north of the museum, you can step inside an *Ultimate Craftsman Bungalow*, built in 1908, that is one of the finest examples of American Arts & Crafts-style architecture.

Museum: $12; free first Fri of month; open Mon & Wed-Thu, noon-5pm; Fri-Sat, 11am-8pm; Sun, 11am-5pm; (626) 449-6840; Metro Rail: Memorial Park *(gold), plus 8 block walk; 411 West Colorado Blvd, Pasadena • House: 1-hour tour $15, on Thu-Fri, 11:30am-4pm & Sat-Sun, noon-4pm. 2-3 hour specialty tours $45-$80, on Mon & Wed (reservation required: GambleHouse.org/tours-visiting) • (626) 793-3334 • 4 Westmoreland Place, Pasadena*

Olvera Street, Avila Adobe & *America Tropical* Mural
(2.5 mi / 2.3 km from LA Arts District)
Join a guided tour along the cobblestone walkways of Olvera Street, the oldest neighborhood in LA, which was founded in 1781 by 11 families of African and Amerindian descent. Then visit six, free museums including Avila Adobe, the oldest home in the city, built in 1818; and *America Tropical (1932)*, David Siqueiros's groundbreaking mural that sparked LA's mural renaissance.

1-Hour Tour: Tue-Sat at 10am, 11am & noon; meet at Tour Office by 501 Los Angeles St • Avila Adobe: 9am-4pm; 10 Olvera St • America Tropical Mural: Tue-Sun, 10am-3pm; bring binoculars; 125 Paseo De La Plaza • Parking $8 at Union Station (below) • Metro Rail: Union Station (gold, red), plus 1 block walk

Union Station
(1.2 mi / 2 km from LA Arts District)
Erected in the 1930s, this is the last great rail station built during the heyday of rail travel in the U.S. It is incredibly well-preserved and was designed to be distinctly Californian—with vaulted ceilings, marble mosaics, Spanish tiles and serene courtyards.

Guided architecture tour: $15; Sat, 10am; duration 2.5 hours; tickets must be purchased in advance via LAConservancy.org or (213) 623-2489 • Parking $8 (East wing) • Metro Rail: Union Station (gold, red) • 800 North Alameda St

Smorgasburg LA
(0.7 mi / 1.2 km from LA Arts District)
Every Sunday, the Alameda Produce Market transforms into an

Kayaking the LA River • The lines, curves and colors of Union Station's original ticket hall

outdoor bazaar where you can indulge in a cornucopia of dishes and sweets—with live music and pop-up boutiques to boot.

Sun, 10am-4pm (ends later in summer) • Some vendors may be cash only • Free 2-hour parking • No pets allowed • 787 Alameda St

Dining Nearby

Bestia
(0.9 mi / 1.4 km from LA Arts District)
Italian ✦ Pasta, pizza, soup, salad, carne, seafood, steak
$25-$85+ • Sun-Thu, 5pm-11pm; Fri-Sat, 5pm-midnight • (213) 514-5724 • 2121 7th Place

Daikokuya
(0.9 mi / 1.4 km from LA Arts District)
Japanese ✦ Ramen, rice bowls, sushi, tempura, carne, seafood
$15-$25+ (cash only) • Mon-Thu, 11am-midnight; Fri-Sat, 11am-1am; Sun, 11am-11pm • (213) 626-1680 • 327 East 1st St

Homegirl Cafe

(1.8 mi / 2.9 km from LA Arts District)
Mexican ♦ Breakfast, chilaquiles, tacos, soup, salad, sandwiches
$15-$20+ • Mon-Fri, 7am-5pm; Sat 9am-2:30pm • (213) 617-0380 • 130 West Bruno St

Urth Caffe

(0.1 mi / 230 m from LA Arts District)
American ♦ Breakfast, coffee, tea, pizza, pastries, salad, sandwiches
$5-$25+ • Sun-Thu, 6am-11pm; Fri-Sat, 6am-midnight • (213) 797-4534 • 451 South Hewitt St

Wurstkuche

(0.5 mi / 750 m from LA Arts District)
German ♦ Sausage, sauerkraut, Belgian fries
$10-$20+ • 11am-1:30am • (213) 687-4444 • 800 East 3rd St

Yxta Cocina Mexicana

(0.4 mi / 700 m from LA Arts District)
Mexican ♦ Soup, salad, sandwiches, tacos, carne, seafood, steak
$20-$70+ • Mon-Tue, 11:30am-9pm; Wed-Fri, 11:30m-10pm; Sat, 4pm-10pm • (213) 596-5579 • 601 South Central Ave

Space Shuttle Endeavour

Feast your eyes upon the Space Shuttle Endeavour, the youngest of the three retired shuttles that ventured to the cosmos and back — numerous times! — during NASA's 30-year space shuttle program.

Planning Guide

In 2012, the Endeavour Shuttle flew into LA, settled into retirement at the California Science Center and has been one of the city's hottest attractions ever since.

During your visit, you will be able to view spacesuits, space capsules and a rocket engine up close...

Gaze upon a lunar rock Buzz Aldrin brought back from the moon in 1969...

And experience what it was like to monitor a live shuttle launch inside the Los Angeles support center that monitored all of NASA's 135 space shuttle launches in tandem with Mission Control in Houston, Texas, and Launch Control in Cape Canaveral, Florida.

More Info	CaliforniaScienceCenter.org	(323) 724-3623
Admission	Free! However, on weekends, holidays and select weekdays, unless you have a ticket to a special exhibit or IMAX film, you must purchase a $2 ticket to view the shuttle at a specific time (purchasable online 3 weeks in advance).
Hours	10am-5pm
Parking	$12, cash only
Metro Rail	Expo Park / USC (Expo line), plus 2 block walk
Map It	700 Exposition Park Dr

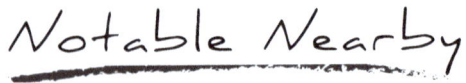

Exposition Park Rose Garden
(Behind the Science Center)
Indulge in a feast for the senses in this 7-acre sunken garden that was planted in 1915, on the site of a 19th century racetrack. The garden boasts over 15,000 rose bushes, across 145 varieties, which are abloom March-Nov; and especially fragrant March-April.

8am-sunset; the garden is closed for pruning Jan 1-Mar 15 • Metro Rail: Expo Park / USC (Expo line), plus 2 block walk • 701 State Dr

NASA Jet Propulsion Laboratory
(18 mi / 29 km away)
Nerd out during a 2-hour guided tour of the JPL campus, where space telescopes, planetary orbiters and Mars rovers are designed and tested before they are rocketed into the Final Frontier.

Free! Advance reservations required: JPL.nasa.gov/events/tours. Tours fill up quickly; luckily, they can be booked 5 months in advance • You must bring a valid government-issued ID with you (non-U.S. citizens must show a passport). A lot of walking is involved, so be sure to wear comfortable shoes and bring a water bottle. • (818) 354-9314 • 4800 Oak Grove Dr, Pasadena

Los Angeles Clippers Basketball
(2.5 mi / 4 km away)
For decades, the Clippers have been overshadowed by the other hometown team, the Los Angeles Lakers. But in recent years, they have undergone a renaissance and are now a team to watch.

Tickets $12-$1,500+ via AXS.com, Ticketmaster.com, StubHub.com and Goldstar.com • Games held Oct-Apr • (213) 742-7340 • Parking $10-$35+ • Metro Rail: Pico (blue, Expo line), plus 2 block walk • 1111 South Figueroa St

Slam dunkin' at a Clippers game • Fleurs in bloom in the Exposition Park Rose Garden

Los Angeles Dodgers Baseball
(5.7 mi / 9.5 km away)
Built in 1962 on the hillside of a natural ravine, this is the third oldest ballpark in the Major Leagues. It is a great place to take in a pro baseball game, since the Dodgers are currently a stellar team that made it to the World Series in 2017.

Tickets $11-$500+ via LosAngeles.dodgers.mlb.com, StubHub.com, SeatGeek.com, BarrysTickets.com and Goldstar.com • Games held Apr-Oct, generally • (866) 363-4377 • Parking $10-$35+ (online); $20-$50+ (at the gate) • Metro Rail: Union Station (gold, red), plus express bus to stadium (bus fare is free if you have a ticket to the game); buses run every 10 min starting 1.5 hours before game time • 1000 Vin Scully Ave

University of Southern California Trojans Football
(0.1 mi / 180 m away)
Get swept up in the youthful energy of an American college football game—cheerleaders dancing; marching bands jamming; and 70,000 students and alumni cheering—in the same stadium where the 1932 and 1984 Summer Olympic games were held.

Tickets $30-$125+ via USCTrojans.com • Games held Sept-Nov • For $40, you can attend a Ralphs tailgate party outside the stadium with food, drinks, *music and revelry 3 hours before game time; or you can attend for free by purchasing $25 of eligible goods at a Ralphs grocery (Ralphs.com/storelocator) that week • (213) 740-4672 • Parking $25+; extremely limited • Metro Rail: Expo Park / USC (Expo line), plus 2 block walk • 3911 South Figueroa St*

Dining Nearby

Chichen Itza

(0.6 mi / 1 km away)
Mexican ◆ Ceviche, tacos, sandwiches, carne, steak, seafood
$15-$25+ • 9am-9pm • (213) 741-1075 • 3655 South Grand Ave, Suite C6

Chick-fil-A

(0.3 mi / 450 m away)
American ◆ Chicken sandwiches, milkshakes, waffle fries, salad
$10+ • Mon-Sat, 8am-11pm • (213) 747-8721 • 3758 South Figueroa St

Figueroa Philly Cheese Steak

(0.3 mi / 400 m away)
American ◆ French fries, onion rings, sandwiches
$15+ • Mon-Fri, 11am-7pm; Sat, 11am-5pm; Sun, noon-5pm • (213) 748-9073 • 3850 South Figueroa St

Jacks N Joe

(1.7 mi / 2.7 km away)
American ◆ Coffee, hash browns, omelets, pancakes, smoothies
$10-$20+ • Mon-Fri, 7am-2pm; Sat-Sun, 8am-2pm • (213) 748-4565 • 2498 South Figueroa St

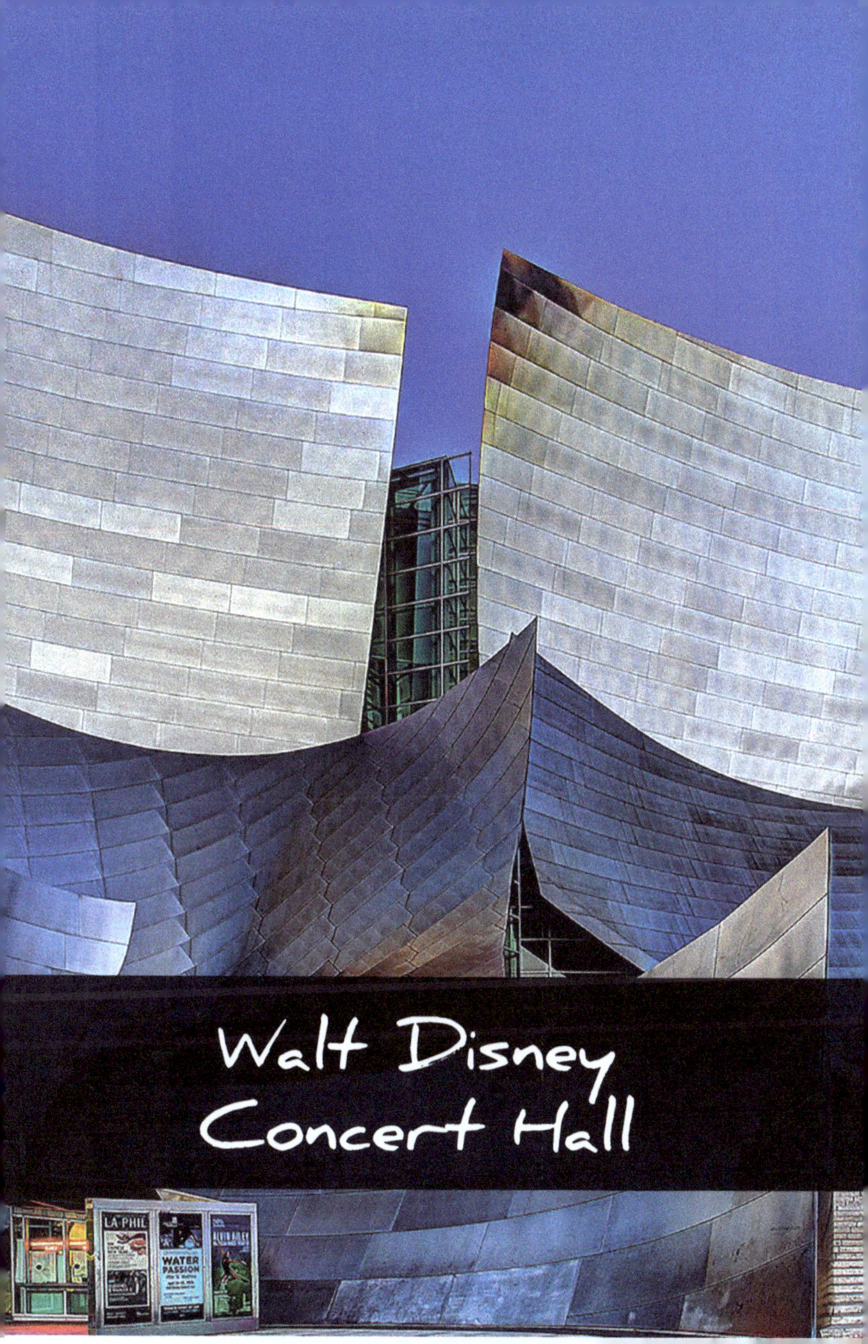
Walt Disney
Concert Hall
LA PHIL
WATER
PASSION

This world-class concert hall, the winter home of the Los Angeles Philharmonic, is iconic for its dramatic exterior. Yet, as the adage goes, it's what's on the inside that counts most. For this is a place not just to behold but, more importantly, to hear — in full symphonic glory.

Planning Guide

The Walt Disney Concert Hall is a definite *Must Hear*... for it was designed by renowned architect, Frank Gehry, to be an acoustical marvel.

The only way to truly appreciate its stunning acoustics is to attend a concert within its wood-paneled walls.

From late September thru early June, the Hall boasts a robust calendar of performances featuring artists and orchestras from around the world; as well as its resident chorus, the Los Angeles Master Chorale, and its permanent orchestra, the LA Philharmonic.

You can choose from an array of genres including classical, jazz, chorales, show tunes and even organ recitals featuring Hurricane

Mama, the Hall's avant-garde pipe organ.

Tickets are available starting in late August. I highly recommend snagging your tickets early as both the best seats and the least expensive seats get snatched up rather quickly.

More Info	LAPhil.com	(323) 850-2000
Tickets	$20-$200+
Tour	Free, guided architecture tours are offered 2-3 days a week. Start times vary; usually between 10am and 1:15pm. Schedules are posted 1-2 months in advance on MusicCenter.org. In most cases, the tour will take you inside the inner concert hall, barring scheduled rehearsals and special events. Call (213) 972-7211 up to 2 weeks beforehand to confirm the inner hall will be accessible on your desired date.
Policies	Use of cameras and recording devices not permitted. Food and drink not allowed inside the Concert Hall. Large bags must be coat checked. Children under age 6 are not admitted to concerts at the hall excepting the Holiday Sing-Along in December for ages 2+.
Parking	$9-$23 (cash only); entrances located on Second St and on Lower Grand Ave. Valet parking $23, with drop off on Hope Ave. Free street parking on Sundays.
Metro Rail	Civic Center / Grand Park (red, purple), plus 2 block walk
Map It	111 South Grand Ave

Insider Tips

★ For optimal sound quality, reserve seats that face the front of the orchestra.

★ Same-day tickets to select shows are available to full-time students and seniors (ages 65+) for only $10-$20; call the box office for availability.

★ DO arrive early. If you arrive after the concert has commenced, you may have to wait until intermission to be escorted to your seat. Note, however, that late seating is not available for concerts that do not have an intermission.

★ DO keep in mind that the hall's acoustics are first-rate and, as such, even the slightest noise—whispering, humming, tapping—can be a significant distraction to all around you. And most importantly, remember to turn off your cell phone.

★ You can get up close and personal with the performers by attending or calling in to a free, pre-concert talk 1 hour before curtain call, for select concerts (to call-in, dial (605) 475-4333 then use access code 184648).

★ During intermission, treat yourself to a stroll in the hall's rooftop garden, which boasts a gorgeous fountain, christened *A Rose for Lilly* (2003), that Gehry designed in tribute to Lillian Disney, Walt Disney's widow, by combining two of her favorite things: roses and Delft Blue china. The garden is freely accessible to the general public via street-level staircases.

★ You can savor fine cuisine on-site at Patina, which La Liste ranked as one of the best restaurants in the U.S. Patina serves up seasonal fare accented with herbs and edible flowers grown in the Hall's rooftop garden (prix fixe $60-$79+ for 3-courses; Sun, 4pm-8pm; Tue-Sat, 5pm-9:30pm). For lighter fare, visit the Concert Hall Cafe ($15-$30+; 9:30am-2pm and, during evening concerts, 5pm-intermission).

Notable Nearby

The Broad

(480 ft / 150 m away)
Beneath the ivory honeycomb facade of LA's newest art museum lies a collection of contemporary art by renowned artists including Jeff Koons, Jean-Michel Basquiat, Andy Warhol and Yayoi Kusama.

Skip the long entry line and reserve a free, timed ticket 1 month in advance via TheBroad.org/visit • Tue-Wed, 11am-5pm; Thu-Fri, 11am-8pm; Sat, 10am-8pm; Sun, 10am-6pm • (213) 232-6200 • Parking $12-$22 • Metro Rail: Civic Center / Grand Park (red, purple), plus 2 block walk • 221 South Grand Ave

Bradbury Building Foyer

(0.5 mi / 800 m away)
Behind the brick facade of Downtown LA's oldest commercial building, built in 1893, lies a gorgeous foyer—of marble staircases, intricate, wrought iron banisters and a glass-domed ceiling—that has starred in many a film including *Blade Runner* and *The Artist*.

Mon-Fri, 9am-6pm; Sat-Sun, 9am-5pm • Parking $2-$24 at 308 South Hill St • Metro Rail: Pershing Square (red, purple), plus 3 block walk • 304 S Broadway

Kara Walker's African't (1996) at The Broad • An indie concert at The Theatre at Ace Hotel

Los Angeles City Hall
(0.5 mi / 0.8 m away)

Enjoy a panoramic view of LA, for free, whilst standing atop this lovely, Byzantine-style building, built in 1928, that has a gorgeous rotunda, topped by a tiled domed, where Prince shot his *Diamonds and Pearls* music video back in the 1990s.

Mon-Fri, 8am-5pm • Bring a government-issued ID • (213) 473-3231 • Parking $8 at 300 East Temple St • Metro Rail: Civic Center / Grand Park (purple, red), plus 2 block walk • 200 North Spring St (public entrance on Main St)

The Theatre at Ace Hotel
(1.2 mi / 2 km away)

Treat yourself to a concert, film, literary reading or theatrical performance at this Gothically-ornate theatre in Downtown LA that is one of the city's great movie palaces from the 1920s.

Tickets via Theatre.AceHotel.com • (213) 235-9614 • Parking $10+ at private lots nearby; on-site valet $30 • Metro Rail: Pershing Square (purple, red), plus 5 block walk • 933 South Broadway

The Wiltern

(4 mi | 6.5 km away)

On the western edge of Koreatown stands the Pellissier, a 12-story, Art Deco building encased in glazed tiles that shimmer like emeralds in the LA sun. The Pellissier is home to The Wiltern, an ornate movie palace from the 1930s wherein you can catch a musical, comedy show or concert with an indie band or a headliner like Adele, Elton John or The Strokes.

Tickets via Wiltern.com • (213) 388-1400 • Parking garage on Oxford St & Wilshire Blvd • Metro Rail: Wilshire / Western (purple) • 3790 Wilshire Blvd

Grand Central Market

(0.4 mi | 700 m away)

In the 1920s, this market was the gastro hub of DTLA, home to 90+ vendors. Nowadays, it is a laid-back foodie bazaar where you can savor a variety of cuisines: from ceviche to currywurst; paella to pupusa; Oaxacan mole to berry galettes.

Sun-Wed, 8am-6pm; Thu-Sat, 8am-9pm • (213) 624-2378 • Parking $2-$24, entrance on 308 South Hill St • Metro Rail: Pershing Square (red, purple), plus 3 block walk • 317 South Broadway

Baco Mercat

(0.7 mi | 1.2 km away)
Mediterranean ◆ Brunch, salad, sandwiches, carne, seafood
$20-$50+ • ☑ Reservations • Mon-Thu, 11:30am-2:30pm & 5:30pm-11pm;

Fri-Sat, 11:30am-3pm & 5:30pm-midnight; Sun, 11:30am-3pm & 5pm-10pm • (213) 687-7000 • 408 South Main St

Bottega Louie

(0.7 mi / 1.2 km away)
Mediterranean ◆ Breakfast, macarons, pizza, seafood, steak
$30-$70+ • Mon-Thu, 6:30am-11pm, Fri, 6:30am-midnight; Sat, 8am-midnight; Sun, 8am-11pm • (213) 802-1470 • 700 South Grand Ave

Nickel Diner

(1 mi / 1.6 km away)
American ◆ Breakfast, burgers, salad, sandwiches, seafood, steak
$15-$30+ • Tue-Sat, 8am-3:30pm & 6pm-10pm; Sun, 8am-3:30pm • (213) 623-8301 • 524 South Main St

Perch

(0.6 mi / 1 km away)

> A ROOFTOP BISTRO WITH LIVE MUSIC NIGHTLY AND 360° VIEWS OF DTLA

French ◆ Brunch, gnocchi, mussels, salad, carne, seafood, steak
$40-$70+ • ☑ Reservations • Mon-Wed, 4pm-1am; Thu-Fri, 4pm-2am; Sat, 11am-2am; Sun, 11am-1am • After 9pm, must be age 21+ • (213) 802-1770 • 448 South Hill St

Q ★

(0.7 mi / 1.1 km away)

> 'ONE OF LA'S 10 BEST RESTAURANTS' – *LOS ANGELES TIMES*

Japanese ◆ Sashimi, sushi, sea urchin, seafood
$85-$175+ • ☑ Reservations • Mon-Thu, noon-2pm & 6:00pm-10pm; Fri, noon-2pm & 6pm-11pm; Sat, 6pm-11pm • (213) 225-6285 • 521 West 7th St

Annual Festivals & Events

 FEB

Modernism Week

Modernism Week is a rare opportunity to go inside some of the beautiful, mid-century modern homes of Palm Springs... where neighbors are constantly competing with each other—spending boatloads on remodels and interior designers—simply for the bragging right of being the 'prettiest house on the block.'

Home tours and/or in-home cocktail parties $45-$375+; tickets available in early Nov: ModernismWeek.com

 APR

Coachella

A 6-day music festival over two weekends that is akin to a hipster Woodstock in a desert utopia of fun, randomness, serendipity and *What happens at Coachella stays at Coachella!* Oh, and the awesome fact that you will get to rock out to a huge lineup of hot artists like Beyonce, Sia, Drake, AC/DC and Kaskade.

Admission wristband $399+ for 1 weekend (Fri-Sun); both weekends have the same music lineup. Early bird wristbands available in early June; the rest in early Jan. They sell out in a heartbeat, so be sure to purchase yours (up to 2) the second they are released on Coachella.com. • 3-day camping pass $113+; must reserve online in advance • 81-800 Avenue 51, Indio

Coachella's dance parties by night 'n day

MAY/JUNE — Balloon & Wine Festival

Lift up with the sunrise during a 3,000-foot (914 m) high hot air balloon ride over Temecula Valley Wine Country, alongside a colorfully serene flock of 50+ balloons. Then partake of wine and beer tastings by day and a Balloon Glow show by night—during which tethered hot air balloons glow in sync to music.

> *1-hour balloon ride + festival pass $210 (Sat-Sun, 6am); 1-Day pass $23-$100+; 3-Day pass $60+ • 3-day RV / tent camping pass $325-$475+ • Tickets and camping passes available in early March via TVBWF.com • 37701 Warren Rd, Winchester*

JULY — Big Bay Boom Fireworks

Beach, barbecue & fireworks! This is how Southern Californians celebrate the 4th of July, America's Independence Day. San Diego's Big Bay Boom is one the biggest and best 4th of July fireworks shows in the country, where you can watch a 17-minute, 180° extravaganza over the city's expansive and glorious bay.

Show begins at 9pm. Come early and claim a spot on the waterfront: BigBayBoom.com/locations; or stay in a hotel room overlooking the bay.

JULY —  Comic-Con

Comic-Con started out in 1970 as a nerd fest for comic book and Sci-Fi enthusiasts. In the decades since, it has super-evolved into the biggest convention in North America, where Hollywood's hottest stars come to roll out trailers, sneak peeks and behind-the-scenes gab; and where fanboys and fangals come to see or be seen in jaw-droppingly elaborate costumes of their favorite Sci-Fi, anime and comic book heroes... and villains!

1-Day admission badge $40-$55+, available in early Jan (note: there is an early bird sale in early Nov that is open to prior attendees only). Badges sell out in a flash, so be sure to purchase yours (up to 3) the second they are released on Comic-Con.org/cci. • 111 W Harbor Dr, San Diego

JULY / AUG —  U.S. Open of Surfing

Watch the world's best surfer dudes and dudettes as they conquer Huntington Beach's infamous waves during this 9-day pro surfing competition that began in 1959 and has since grown into the world's largest, replete with pro skateboard and BMX competitions, fashion shows, rock concerts and more.

Free! • VansUSOpenofSurfing.com • 325 Pacific Coast Hwy, Huntington Beach

The Blue Angels in daredevil formation at the Miramar Air Show • Balloons on parade at the Temecula Valley Balloon & Wine Festival

Miramar Air Show

Welcome to the Danger Zone! Where Charles Lindbergh conducted test runs before his historic solo flight across the Atlantic in 1927; where real-life TOPGUN Navy pilots trained in the 1970s-90s; and where scenes were filmed for the movie, *Top Gun*. Nowadays, Miramar is home to the largest military air show in the U.S., where you can watch Navy pilots, Army paratroopers and civilian jet teams doing death-defying stunts that will take your breath away.

Free! • Bring your own folding chair or blanket to sit on; or reserve grandstand seating for $30-$300+ via MiramarAirShow.com • You must have your driver's license, car registration (or rental car agreement) and proof of car insurance on-hand to drive onto the military base where the event is held • East Gate: Miramar Way & Kearny Villa Rd, San Diego

Eatin' Good in SoCal!

Grilled Seafood Tacos

Grilled fish tacos and grilled shrimp tacos are a healthy, SoCal twist on the fried seafood tacos that Southern Californians indulge in whenever they visit Mexico's Baja Peninsula.

Traditionally, the dish is a flavorful feast of freshly grilled fish or shrimp placed on a bed of corn tortillas then sprinkled with cabbage and pico de gallo, drizzled with a white sauce and spritzed with fresh lime.

Ironically enough, an excellent place to enjoy a grilled seafood taco is in the desert—at Shanghai Reds Bar & Grill in Palm Springs.

$10+ • Mon-Thu, 5pm-10pm; Fri, 5pm-11:30pm; Sat, 11am-4pm & 5pm-11:30pm; Sun, 11am-4pm & 5pm-10pm • Live music Thu-Sat nights; happy hour specials all-day Sun & after 8pm, Mon-Sat • (760) 322-9293 • 235 South Indian Canyon Dr, Palm Springs

Boysenberry

It is not everyday you can savor a berry that gave rise to a billion dollar theme park empire.

Back before Knott's Berry Farm grew into Southern California's first theme park, it was a modest berry farm that specialized in the boysenberry—a blackberry, raspberry and loganberry hybrid that was cultivated in Orange County in 1924.

People would wait for hours just to get a helping of Mrs. Knott's boysenberry pie, punch, jam and sherbet.

In 1941, Mr. Knott added a Wild West Ghost Town to keep customers entertained during their wait. Over time, he kept adding attractions and the Ghost Town grew into a popular theme park—years before Disneyland debuted in 1955, just a few miles down the road.

Nowadays, you can treat yourself to Mrs. Knott's boysenberry pie and other boysenberry delights at the California Marketplace located outside the park.

$5-$15+ • Knotts.com/things-to-do/california-marketplace • Free 3-hour parking with proof of purchase • If you want to ride the roller coasters and thrill rides in the theme park, save 40% by buying your ticket on Knotts.com for just $44+; theme park parking $18 • 8039 Beach Blvd, Buena Park

Certified Farmers Markets

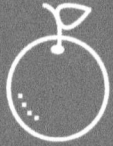

Up until the 1950s, Southern California was such an agricultural powerhouse that one of its counties christened itself Orange County in 1889. Nowadays, the OC still grows $64 million worth of produce a year, with strawberries as its top crop.

Meanwhile, its neighbor to the south, San Diego County, has more farms than any other county in the U.S., and it grows an astounding $565 million worth of produce every year, with lemons and Hass avocados as its top crops.

You can savor this harvest at a Certified Farmers Market (CFM), where you can also discover eats and treats by local chefs and take home unique finds crafted by local artists and artisans.

★ Bring cash; some vendors do not accept credit cards.

★ Bring a reusable bag or two to carry all of your goodies in.

★ Arrive early so you will have first dibs on the best produce.

Disneyland

Wednesday	8am-1pm	**Fullerton CFM** 801 West Valencia Dr, Fullerton *4 mi l 6.5 km away*
Thursday	11am-4pm	**Downtown Anaheim CFM** 205 Center Street Promenade, Anaheim *2.5 mi l 4.5 km away*
Saturday	9am-1pm	**Old Town Orange CFM** 304 North Cypress St, Orange *6 mi l 9.5 km away*
	9am-2pm	**Buena Park CFM** 8150 La Palma Ave, Buena Park *6 mi l 9.5 km away*
Sunday	9am-2pm	**Garden Grove CFM** Main St & Garden Grove Blvd *4 mi l 6.5 km away*

Indian Canyon Oases

Wednesday	8am-12:30pm	**Palm Desert CFM** 72559 CA-111, Palm Desert *12 mi l 21 km away*
Saturday	8am-12:30pm	**Palm Springs CFM** 2300 East Baristo Rd, Palm Springs *5 mi l 8 km away*

North County, San Diego

Tuesday	10am-2pm	**Univ. of Califoria, San Diego CFM**
		Library Walk & Lyman Way, La Jolla
		*6 mi	9.5 km from Windansea Beach*
Wednesday	3pm-6pm	**Carlsbad State Street CFM**
		State Street & Carlsbad Village Dr
		*10.5 mi	17 km from Swami's Beach*
	5pm-7pm	**Encinitas Station CFM**
		600 South Vulcan Ave, Encinitas
		*0.6 mi	1 km from Swami's Beach*
Thursday	9am-1pm & 5pm-9pm	**Oceanside CFM**
		Pier View Way & Coast Hwy, Oceanside
		*14 mi	22.5 km from Swami's Beach*
Saturday	1pm-4pm	**Del Mar CFM**
		1050 Camino del Mar, Del Mar
		*0.6 mi	1 km from Del Mar Beach*
Sunday	9am-1pm	**La Jolla CFM**
		Girard Ave & Genter St, La Jolla
		*1 mi	1.6 km from Windansea Beach*
	10am-2pm	**Leucadia CFM**
		185 Union St, Encinitas
		*1.8 mi	3 km from Swami's Beach*

Disneyland

Spend a day or two at the Happiest Place on Earth, where you can share a hug with your favorite Disney characters; watch parades, fireworks and live shows; and delight in over 80 rides including Star Tours, Mad Tea Cups, Splash Mountain and Pirates of the Caribbean.

Planning Guide

There's no place like Disneyland, a land of magic and wonder that holds a special place in many a Southern Californian's heart.

Since 1955, Disney's first theme park has grown into a resort with two parks, three resort hotels and Downtown Disney, a dining and shopping plaza. The two parks, Disneyland and California Adventure, are both filled with rides, live shows, parades, art exhibits, shops and a variety of cuisine options for every budget.

Each park is divided into distinctly themed lands that are fully immersive steps into the past... the future... or a land of whimsy and fantasy:

Disneyland	California Adventure
Adventureland	"a bug's land"
Critter Country	Buena Vista Street
Fantasyland	Cars Land
Frontierland	Grizzly Peak
Main Street, U.S.A.	Hollywood Land
Mickey's Toontown	Pacific Wharf
New Orleans Square	Paradise Pier
Tomorrowland	

If you are a first-time visitor, I recommend spending at least one day in each park, as there is much to see and do in both.

However, if you are a huge fan of all things Disney, additional days would be ideal as it would give you time to ride most of the rides in each park and to catch most of the shows and parades.

Alternatively, if you have only one day to spare, you can do just Disneyland Park; or you can buy a Park Hopper ticket to visit both Disneyland and California Adventure in the same day (both park's entrances are within walking distance of each other).

I highly recommend buying park tickets and booking table-service dining reservations online in advance, so you can better enjoy your visit to the *Happiest Place on Earth*.

More Info	Disneyland.com	(714) 782-4636
Tickets	1-Day ticket $97-$124+. Multi-day tickets available at a discounted rate. To visit both parks on the same day, you must purchase a 1-Day Park Hopper ticket, which is $157-$174+. Entry to Downtown Disney is free.
Hours	Vary by season, generally 8am-10pm (closes later in summer); hours are posted online 12 months before
Policies	The following are not permitted: outside food or beverages; glass; selfie sticks; pets; skates; skateboards; bags on wheels; bags or coolers larger than 18"x25"x37" (45x63x93 cm)
Parking	$20+; available 90 minutes before the parks open. Downtown Disney parking is free for the first 3 hours.

Clockwise: Mickey and friends with the Disneyland Band in front of Sleeping Beauty Castle • Picture perfect waves in Crystal Cove State Park• And they're off on the California Screamin' roller coaster • The lush gardens at the historic Mission San Juan Capistrano

LA Metro Rail + Bus	7th St / Metro Center (purple, red) in DTLA, then walk 1.5 blocks to corner of South Flower St & 6th St and catch Bus 460 direct to the park; takes appx. 2 hours. Bus runs 4:30am (southbound) - 2am (northbound)
Map It	1313 Disneyland Dr, Anaheim

Disneyland
Like a Pro

One of the biggest time sucks at Disneyland is waiting in line.

Waiting in line to buy park tickets (which is why you should definitely buy yours online). Waiting to be seated for a live show... to take a picture with one of your favorite Disney characters... and worst yet, to ride some of the more popular attractions, with wait times often soaring past 90 minutes.

Luckily, there are 4 ways you can decrease your wait time for certain rides:

Zip to the Front with FASTPASS

Each of the following attractions has a FASTPASS distribution kiosk where you can get a free FASTPASS ticket that will have a time window on it. Later, when you return to the attraction within that time window,

you will be able to join a fast-moving line that will have you on the ride in no time. Also, once the time window begins for one FASTPASS, you are eligible to get a FASTPASS at a different ride... and so on... and so on...!

Disneyland	California Adventure
Big Thunder Mountain Railroad	California Screamin'
Buzz Lightyear Astro Blasters	Goofy's Sky School
Haunted Mansion *(Sept-early Jan)*	Grizzly River Run
Indiana Jones Adventure	Radiator Springs Racers
Roger Rabbit's Car Toon Spin	Soarin' Around the World
Space Mountain	Star Tours
Splash Mountain	

Hop into a Single Rider Line

Each of the following attractions has a Single Rider line via which you can fill an empty seat on the ride when one is available. The Single Rider line moves 2 to 4 times faster than the main line.

Sometimes it can be hard to spot the entrance for the Single Rider line, so, when in doubt, go to the entrance of the attraction where there is usually a Cast Member (employee) nearby who can point you in the right direction.

Disneyland	California Adventure
Indiana Jones Adventure	California Screamin'
Matterhorn Bobsleds	Goofy's Sky School
Splash Mountain	Grizzly River Run
	Radiator Springs Racers

Wield Wait Times in the Palm of Your Hand

Before you visit the park, download the official Disneyland app (on iOS or Android) to your smartphone so you can easily check ride wait times and character photo op locations while on-the-go in the parks.

There is no public wifi in the parks, so you will need to be connected to a cellular data network to utilize the app.

Stay at a Disneyland Resort Hotel

By staying at the Grand Californian Hotel & Spa *($400+)*, Disneyland Hotel *($350+)* or Paradise Pier Hotel *($250+)*, you can enter the parks 1 hour before they open to the general public. This is the best way to ride popular rides with little to no wait.

If your budget can swing it, I highly suggest staying at the Grand Californian. Not only is it a lovely hotel, with the look and feel of a luxury mountain lodge, but it also boasts guest-only entrances direct into California Adventure and Downtown Disney.

Another benefit of staying in a resort hotel is that, when you are shopping in the parks or Downtown Disney, you can have your purchases delivered straight to your room.

Insider Tips

★ The least crowded time to visit the parks is on a Tuesday, Wednesday or Thursday during January, February and May.

★ A special, albeit crowded, time to visit is in the fall when the parks are decked out for Halloween in September and October; and as a Winter Wonderland in November and December.

★ Wait times for most rides tend to go down dramatically when a parade or fireworks show is in progress.

★ In search of an affordable hotel room near the parks? I suggest staying at a hotel that is along the Anaheim Resort Transportation (ART) bus route so you can take a bus to Disneyland and forgo having to pay $18 for parking. Bus fare is $5 for 1 day; $12 for 3 days; $20 for 5 days. You can view a list of eligible hotels on RideArt.org.

★ If it is your first time visiting Disneyland, or if you are celebrating a birthday, graduation, engagement, wedding or anniversary, you can get a free, commemorative button at City Hall in Disneyland and at Guest Relations in California Adventure, both of which are located near the entrance of each park, on your left.

Notable Nearby

Huntington Beach
(20 mi / 33 km away)
A popular surfer's beach, especially near the pier, that boasts a wide and sandy shore hugged by a long, scenic bike path, as well as a nearby main street with beachy keen shops and eateries.
Lifeguards: 10am-sunset • Food concessions, restrooms, showers, firepits, bike rentals • Parking $1.50-$15 • 325 Pacific Coast Hwy, Huntington Beach

Mission San Juan Capistrano
(30 mi / 48 km away)
Get a fascinating glimpse into what life was like for California's first European settlers at this Catholic mission built in 1776. The gardens and grounds are so beautiful and serene, it is easy to see why it is regarded as the *Jewel* of the 21 missions that were erected when *Alta California* was a Spanish colony in 1769–1823.
Admission $9 • 9am-5pm • (949) 234-1300 • Train: San Juan Capistrano Station (Amtrak, Metrolink), plus 1.5 block walk • 26801 Ortega Highway, San Juan Capistrano

South Coast Plaza & Segerstrom Center for the Arts
(11.5 mi / 18.5 km away)
Shop and dine at this luxurious mall that is home to delicious restaurants and 250+ boutiques including Dolce & Gabbana and PRADA. Then treat yourself to a performance at the Segerstrom nearby, with artists and plays like Michael Bolton and *Rent*.
Plaza: Mon-Fri, 10am-9pm; Sat, 10am-8pm; Sun, 11am-6:30pm; 3333 Bristol St, Costa Mesa • Segerstrom: For tickets and showtimes, visit SCFTA.org; (714) 556-2787; 600 Town Center Dr, Costa Mesa

Anaheim Ducks Hockey

(4 mi / 7 km away)

Watch the mighty Ducks, one of the top professional hockey teams in the U.S., live and in action October thru April.

Tickets $12-$700+ via Ticketmaster.com, StubHub.com and Goldstar.com • (714) 704-2500 • Parking $20+ • Train: Anaheim Station (Amtrak, Metrolink), plus 3 block walk • 2695 East Katella Ave, Anaheim

Crystal Cove State Park

(25 mi / 40 km away)

Lovely and secluded, this nature park boasts sandy coves, tide pools, hiking and biking trails, a restaurant, campsites and seaside cottages that were built in the 1930s.

Tent / RV camping $50-$75+; cottages $30-$200+; both are reservable 7 months in advance via ReserveCalifornia.com • (949) 494-3539 • Day use parking $15 (6am-sunset) • 8471 North Coast Hwy, Laguna Beach

* Valid theme park admission ticket required

Cafe Orleans

(In Disneyland Park*, New Orleans Square)
Creole ✦ Beignets, crepes, gumbo, salad, carne, seafood
$25-$40+ • ☑ Reservations • 11:30am-8pm • (714) 781-3463

Carthay Circle Restaurant

(In California Adventure Park*, Buena Vista Street)
American ✦ Burgers, ceviche, salad, pasta, carne, duck, seafood

$35-$60+ • ☑ Reservations • 11:30am-3:30pm & 4:30pm-9:30pm • (714) 781-3463

Earl of Sandwich
(In Downtown Disney)
American ◆ Breakfast, soup, salad, sandwiches, wraps
$10+ • 8am-midnight, generally • (714) 817-7476 • 1565 Disneyland Dr, Anaheim

Napa Rose
(In Grand Californian Hotel & Spa)
American ◆ Soup, salad, octopus, carne, seafood, steak, veal
$60+ • ☑ Reservations • 5:30pm-9:15pm • (714) 781-3463 • 1600 Disneyland Dr, Anaheim

Steakhouse 55
(In Disneyland Hotel)
American ◆ Breakfast, soup, salad, lobster, carne, seafood, steak
$20-$60+ • ☑ Reservations • 7am-11am & 5:30pm-10pm • (714) 781-3463 • 1150 West Magic Way, Anaheim

Anaheim Packing District
(2.5 mi / 4 km away)
From 1919-1955, local farmers would bring their freshly-picked citrus to the Packing House for washing and shipping. Nowadays, the House is home to 20+ bars, cafes and restaurants serving up a mouthwatering array of inventive cuisine: from Southern seafood to gelato on a stick.

9am-midnight • Live music on select days: AnaheimPackingDistrict.com/calendar/events • 440 South Anaheim Blvd, Anaheim

Indian Canyon Oases

Relish the beauty and serenity of the California desert in a trio of canyons on Cahuilla Indian tribal land, where you can stroll beneath a canopy of the world's largest oasis of desert fan palms, the only palm tree that is native to California.

3 Ways to 'Lawrence of Arabia' in the Canyons

Andreas Canyon

Enjoy a picnic under a canopy of palms before embarking on the 1.2 mile (1.9 km) Andreas Canyon Loop Trail.

During much of the trail, you will be walking alongside a perennial stream brimming with flora and fauna.

The trail is so scenic and serene, you will emerge feeling rejuvenated and in awe of nature's beauty and bounty.

Murray Canyon

Journey past seasonal creeks and through the open desert as you hike 4.7 miles (7.6 km), roundtrip, to the Seven Sisters Waterfall, where you can cool off with an invigorating swim.

Generally, the best time to visit the falls is March thru May, as the snow melts atop mountains nearby. The Murray Canyon Trail is easy-to-moderate, and since much of the trail is bereft of shade, the best time of day to hike it is in the coolness of the morn.

Palm Canyon

Stand under the awesome coolness of the world's largest grove of desert fan palms, the only palm tree that is actually native to California.

On weekends, you can join a 1 mile (1.6 km) ranger-led hike during which you will learn about the Cahuilla tribe and how their ancestors thrived here for hundreds of years.

Planning Guide

The Indian Canyon Oases are a 2-hour drive east from Los Angeles. The road trip is a fascination unto itself as LA's crisscross of gritty freeways gives way to cookie-cutter suburbia and then to the arid poetry of the California desert.

The best time to visit is during the cooler months, November thru March, when daytime temperatures are a more bearable 69°- 80° F (21°-27° C.).

I suggest spending 1 to 2 days exploring the canyons. After your hike, you can overnight in the small city of Palm Springs.

Or, better yet, in the nearby town of Desert Hot Springs (15 mi | 24 km north), which boasts over a dozen day spas and resort hotels where you can relax in natural hot or cold mineral springs. For a list of spas and hotels: VisitDesertHotSprings.com

More Info	Indian-Canyons.com	(760) 323-6018
Admission	$9 (Oct-Jun); $5 (July-Sept)
Hours	Oct-June: 8am-5pm; July-Sept: Fri-Sun only, 8am-5pm
Ranger Hikes	Palm Canyon: Fri-Sun, 10am; Andreas Canyon: Fri-Sun, 1pm
Ranger Talks	Palm Canyon: Mon-Thu, 10am (Oct-May)	Andreas Canyon: Mon-Thu, 1pm (Oct-May)
Policies	Hiking is permitted on designated trails only. The following are not permitted: overnight camping or backpacking; fires; smoking; pets; alcoholic beverages; bicycles on trails; rock climbing; firearms; fireworks; vandalism; loud noises or music; removal or destruction of plants, rocks, cultural objects, etc.
Train + Bus	From Downtown LA (Union Station), take a 3-4 hour train + bus trip via Amtrak to the Palm Springs Airport where you can rent a car or hire a taxi for the 6 mi (9.5 km) drive to the oases.
Map It	38500 South Palm Canyon Dr, Palm Springs

Insider Tips

★ The city of Palm Springs is a popular destination and often has festivals and events during which every single hotel will be sold out. I highly suggest making hotel reservations far in advance.

★ In and around the canyons, there are a number of other hiking trails you can explore. For trail maps and recommendations, visit the Trading Post (visitors center) located next to the Palm Canyon parking lot.

★ Stay hydrated at all times while in the desert. And follow the rule of thumb that during a wilderness hike, when half of your water is gone, it is time to start heading back to civilization. You should also drink plenty of water the night before your hike and refrain from consuming alcohol.

★ The desert sun can be much more taxing and dangerous than you think. Hiking during the heat of a hot day is NOT at all wise. On warm days, I suggest wearing breathable pants, a long-sleeved shirt, wide hat, sunscreen and lip balm.

★ Before embarking on a long hike, be sure to pack a trail map, compass, first aid kit and water.

★ DO NOT visit the canyons if there is a chance of rain in the forecast. Flash floods can occur and being caught in one could result in death.

★ This is rattlesnake country. So stay alert and if you encounter a snake in your path, pass it with caution.

★ If hiking alone, be sure to let someone (friend, park ranger, etc.) know what your route is and when you plan to return.

★ Pay it forward, leave no trace. Help keep this and all of earth's natural wonders beautiful and pristine!

Notable Nearby

Joshua Tree National Park
(Visitors Center 39 mi / 62 km away)
Climb atop bulbous rocks, hike through slot canyons and marvel at eponymous Joshua trees—large, spiky yucca plants native only to the American Southwest—whose limbs often seem to be in the midst of an interpretive dance.

Admission $25 per vehicle (good for 7 days) • Tent / RV camping $15-20; 2 campgrounds are reservable Oct-May via Recreation.gov; 7 other camps are first-come, year-round • (760) 367-5500 • 6554 Park Blvd, Joshua Tree

Sky Art of Borrego Springs
(89 mi / 143 km away)
Escape to an arid land where you can commune with dinosaurs, camels, saber-toothed cats and a 350-foot (107 km) Oriental serpent as it crosses the road! Borrego Springs is home to over 130 life-sized, metal sculptures of creatures ranging from the prehistoric to the fantastical—all the commissioned work of

The rock formations and prickly flora of Joshua Tree • Desert bighorn sheep just hangin' out in Anza-Borrego Desert State Park

Ricardo Breceda, a self-taught artist based in Southern California.

Begin your self-guided driving tour at the Anza-Borrego Desert State Park Visitors Center (address below; Oct-May: 9am-5pm; June-Sept: Sat-Sun only, 9am-5pm) where you can pick up a free map of the sculptures' locations. The tour is mostly on paved roads and approximately 22 miles (35 km) roundtrip.

Anza-Borrego Desert State Park
(Visitors Center 90 mi / 145 km away)

Explore canyons, palm groves and badlands whilst spying bighorn sheep, roadrunners, iguanas and more in this remote wilderness that is especially resplendent in March when its desert sands are blanketed with wildflowers. Highlights include the 3-mile (4.8 km), roundtrip, Palm Canyon Trail and Font's Point overlook.

Day use parking $5, open dawn to dusk • Tent/RVCamping $20-$35+; reservable via ReserveCalifornia.com at least 2 days in advance • To discover what wildflowers are presently in bloom, call the Wildflower Hotline: (760) 767-4684 • Visitors Center: (760) 767-4205 • 300 Palm Canyon Dr, Borrego Springs

Palm Springs Air Museum

(8 mi | 13 km away)

Sit in the cockpit of a bona fide World War II fighter plane and step inside a B-17 bomber at this air museum that is home to the largest collection of flyable WWII planes in the world.

Admission $16.50 • 10am-5pm • Cockpit photo ops on Sat, 10:30am-12:30pm • (760) 778-6262 • 745 North Gene Autry Trail, Palm Springs

Palm Springs Aerial Tramway

(11 mi | 18 km away)

Escape the heat and ascend 6,000 ft (1.8 km) to the pine forests, hiking trails and campsites atop Mount San Jacinto, via the world's largest rotating tramway. Along the way, enjoy hawkish views of the picturesque Coachella Valley below.

Tickets $24.95 • First tram: Mon-Fri, 10am; Sat-Sun, 8am; Fri (July-Sept), 8am; closed for maintenance latter half of Sept • Backcountry camping: $5 wilderness permit required, available at ranger station atop the mountain (by the tram station) • Parking $5 • (888) 515-8726 • 1 Tram Way, Palm Springs

Dining Nearby

Cheeky's

(6 mi | 10 km away)

American ✦ Breakfast, burgers, sandwiches, carne

$15-$20+ • Thu-Mon, 8am-2pm • (760) 327-7595 • 622 North Palm Canyon Dr, Palm Springs

Elmer's Restaurant

(3.5 mi / 5.5 km away)
American ◆ Breakfast, burgers, salad, sandwiches, seafood, steak
$15-$30+ • ☑ Reservations • 6am-9pm • (760) 327-8419 • 1030 East Palm Canyon Dr, Palm Springs

Great Shakes

(5.5 mi / 9 km away)
Snack ◆ Milkshakes, malts, ice cream floats
$5+ • Sun-Wed, noon-9pm; Thu-Fri, noon-10pm; Sat, noon-11pm • (760) 327-5300 • 160 South Palm Canyon Dr, Palm Springs

Le Vallauris

(5.5 mi / 9 km away)
Mediterranean ◆ Brunch, duck, lobster salad, carne, seafood, steak
$44-$100+ • Fri-Sun, 11:30am-2:30pm & 5pm-10:30pm; Mon-Thu, 5pm-10:30pm • (760) 325-5059 • 385 West Tahquitz Canyon Way, Palm Springs

Sherman's Deli & Bakery

(4.5 mi / 7.5 km away)
American ◆ Breakfast, pasta, salad, sandwiches, soup, carne, steak
$20-$30+ • 7am-9pm • (760) 325-1199 • 401 East Tahquitz Canyon Way, Palm Springs

Trio

(5.5 mi / 8.5 km away)
American ◆ Brunch, burgers, salad, sandwiches, seafood, steak
$30-$60+ • ☑ Reservations • Mon-Thu, 11am-10pm; Fri, 11am-11pm; Sat, 10am-11pm; Sun, 10am-10pm • (760) 864-8746 • 707 North Palm Canyon Dr, Palm Springs

North County, San Diego

San Diego is California's oldest and southernmost city; and its north coastal suburbs are home to gorgeous beaches and laid-back beach towns, where you can surf or beach bum by day; and imbibe on local craft beer and fish tacos by night... and day!

3 Gorgeous Shores for Beach Bliss

Situated 1.5 hours south of Los Angeles, the North County coastline stretches on for 40 miles (64 km) and encompasses five beach towns—Oceanside, Carlsbad, Encinitas, Solana Beach and Del Mar—as well as the tony neighborhood of La Jolla.

Individually, they each have their own unique vibe of *lazy-faire*. And collectively, they are home to over a dozen lovely state and city beaches.

Yet, there are three beaches in particular that stand out amongst the rest as North County's most YOLO-worthy stretches of sand and sea:

Windansea Beach, La Jolla

Windansea is breathtakingly gorgeous. One look upon its emerald and turquoise waves, and you will be overcome with desire—the desire to dive in and frolic with wanton abandon, from dawn till dusk.

Windansea is a popular surfing and boogie boarding hangout. The beach itself is not considerably wide, but it is longer than it at first appears. So if the main stretch of sand is packed, just walk towards a maze of boulders where you may luck out on a small yet semi-private spot to relax and repose during low tide.

> *Lifeguards on duty 9am-sunset (June-Aug); and on warm days the rest of the year • Smoking, glass containers, littering, alcoholic beverages, loud music, disturbing noises, overnight camping and dogs are not permitted • Limited street parking is available on Neptune Place and neighboring streets; on summer weekends (June-Sept) and holidays, arrive early to snag a spot • 6946 Neptune Place, La Jolla*

Del Mar Beach

Del Mar is a glorious and expansive beach that hugs the coast for 2 miles.

You can go for a jog along the shore when the sun is low; walk over to quaint shops and seaside restaurants nearby; or lounge under a beach umbrella for hours without a care in the world.

And, if feeling a bit adventurous, you can hike an unofficial trail on the bluffs at the beach's southern end, where you can enjoy elevated views of one of California's prettiest beaches.

A picture-perfect low tide along the northern stretch of Swami's Beach

> Lifeguards on duty 9am-sunset • Restrooms; beach volleyball courts. Outdoor showers turned off due to statewide drought. • Alcoholic beverages are banned Mar-early Sept. Dogs allowed only on north end of the beach (north of 29th St). Smoking, glass containers, fires, tents and overnight camping not permitted. • On summer weekends (June-Sept) and holidays, lot and street parking can be impossible to come by; arrive super early (7am-8am) or take public transportation • Train + Metro Bus: from Solana Beach Station, take the 101 bus to Camino Del Mar & 15th St; and walk 2 blocks to the beach. • *1658 Coast Blvd, Del Mar*

Swami's Beach, Encinitas

Swami's is a beauty.

It has the look and feel of a deserted island in paradise, with the added bonus that it is a popular snorkeling spot and a surfing mecca where, on days when the surf's up, you can watch top-notch amateur surfers catching waves with aplomb.

Lifeguards on duty 8am-sunset (mid June-Aug); weekends only (Sept-May) • Restrooms on left side of parking lot; outdoor shower under staircase on beach • Smoking, alcoholic beverages, glass containers, fires, skateboards and dogs not permitted • On summer weekends, holidays and days when surf conditions are ripe, parking can be extremely hard to come by, so arrive early or take public transportation • Train + Metro Bus: Encinitas Station, then take the 101 bus to South Coast Hwy & Swami's Pedestrian Xing (by a temple with gold domes shaped like lotus bulbs). Walk 1 block south to a parking lot where you can take stairs down to the beach. • 1298 South Coast Highway, Encinitas

Insider Tips

★ The best time to visit is July thru September, when the air and ocean temperatures will be at their warmest.

★ North County is delightfully accessible via Amtrak's Pacific Surfliner train, which makes stops at Union Station in LA, Anaheim Station near Disneyland, Solana Beach Station near Del Mar, Encinitas Station near Swami's and the Santa Fe Depot in downtown San Diego. For tickets: Amtrak.com.

★ In early summer, many beaches in California experience a phenomena called May Gray and June Gloom, wherein during the morning, the skies are blanketed in a gray marine layer that makes it seem as though a rainstorm is imminent. But this is simply a coastal fog that will lift around noon, at which point the glorious California sun will regale you with its sunny disposition for the remainder of the day!

★ DO NOT swim or surf in the ocean 3 to 5 days after a rainstorm as there is likely to be debris and bacteria, washed in from nearby storm drains, that could cause injury or illness.

★ Some North County beaches experience rip currents—very strong waves close to shore that can carry you out to sea. If you get caught in one, swim parallel to the ocean until you are out of the current. Before getting in the ocean, ask a lifeguard if there are any rip currents nearby.

★ Pay it forward, leave no trace. Help keep these gorgeous beaches beautiful and pristine!

Notable Nearby

La Jolla Sea Caves & Ecological Reserve
(2.8 mi / 4.4 km from Windansea Beach)
Embark on a kayak and snorkel safari in this ecological reserve where you can marvel at the landscapes that inspired Dr. Seuss—who once lived on the cliffs above—whilst having fun encounters with seals, sea lions, leopard sharks and more.
2-hour kayak cave tour $45-$79; 2-hour sunset tour $59-$89; 2-hour kayak and snorkel tour $69-$109 • LaJollaKayak.com/tours

Torrey Pines Gliderport
(6 mi / 10 km from Windansea Beach)
The Torrey Pines State Natural Reserve is heralded as one of the best places to glide in North America, thanks to optimal

winds year-round and breathtaking views of the nature reserve, its hiking trails and its world-class surfer's beach, Blacks Beach.

Tandem paragliding $175 or hang gliding $225 for 20-25 minutes; walk-in only (call before to confirm flights are 'a go' that day) • 9am-5pm • (858) 452-9858 • 2800 Torrey Pines Scenic Dr, La Jolla • If you want to hike or beach bum in the nature reserve nearby, day use parking $4-$15 (8am-sunset); 12600 North Torrey Pines Rd, La Jolla

USS Midway Aircraft Carrier

(15 mi | 24 km from Windansea Beach)

Step onto a WWII-era U.S. warship that was the largest ship in the world when it first set sail in 1945. Via a self-guided audio tour, you can explore the engine room, mess hall, sleeping quarters and the flight deck, where you can sit in the cockpit of a fighter jet!

Admission $18-$20 • 10am-5pm • (619) 544-9600 • Parking $10 • Train: Santa Fe Depot (Amtrak), plus 4 block walk • 910 North Harbor Dr, San Diego

Balboa Park & California Tower

(13 mi | 22 km from Windansea Beach)

Get a 360° view of the nation's largest urban cultural park and the city of San Diego whilst standing atop California Tower. This 198-foot (60 m) tower is an architectural remnant of a 1915 World's Fair, which debuted a cadre of ornate buildings that sparked the Spanish Colonial Revival movement that has inspired the design of homes and buildings in California for over a century, including Beverly Hills City Hall and the infamous Hearst Castle.

California Tower: 40-minute tour $22.50 (includes admission to the Museum of Man): MuseumofMan.org/tickets; 1350 El Prado • Free guided tours of the Park's gardens and buildings: Tue & Sun, 11am-noon; meet at the Visitors Center (1549 El Prado, San Diego; (619) 239-0512) • 1.5-hour audio tour $5, available at the Visitors Center • On Sat-Sun and holidays, free parking can be hard to find; come early or take the 7 bus or 215 bus from Sante Fe Depot

The century-old California Tower holding court o'er Balboa Park • Gliding away o'er Torrey Pines State Natural Reserve

Hotel del Coronado & Silver Strand State Beach
(18 mi / 28 km away from Windansea Beach)
Ferry across San Diego's illustrious bay to the Coronado Peninsula, where you can bike along the coast for 3 miles (5 km) to the white sand beaches of the Hotel del Coronado, a gorgeous, Queen-Anne style resort built in the 1880s. Enjoy a 90-minute, guided tour of this historic hotel before riding south for 5.5 miles (8.8 km) to Silver Strand State Beach, via The Strand, a scenic road flanked by the ocean on one side and the bay on the other.

Ferry: 15-minute ride via Flagship Ferry; departs from Broadway Pier (990 N Harbor Dr, San Diego) hourly from 9am-9pm; $9.50 roundtrip; park at USS Midway (p 145) or take the train to Santa Fe Depot (Amtrak) and walk 2 blocks • At the Coronado Ferry Landing, you can rent a bike for $8+/hour or $29+/day • Bike path map: TheYOLOGuide.com/california/coronado-map • Hotel: 1500 Orange Ave, Coronado; (619) 435-6611; 1.5 hour guided tour $20 on Mon, Wed & Fri, 10:30am & Sat-Sun, 2pm; reservable via CoronadoHistory.org • State Beach: 5000 CA Route 75, Coronado. Day use parking $8-$10, 7am-7pm (open till 8pm, Mar-May; 9pm, June-Aug). RV camping $50-$65, reservable 7 months in advance via ReserveAmerica.com.

Temecula Valley Wine Country
(48 mi l 77 km away from Swamis Beach)
Discover delightful Southern California wines and gaze upon rolling hills of vine during a tasting tour in the Temecula Valley, which is home to 30+ wineries including Callaway and Vindemia, award-winning vintners of premium Zinfandel, California's signature winegrape for over a century.

Callaway Winery: Tasting $15; winery tour + tasting $25; 10am-5pm (tours at 11am & 1pm); (951) 676-4001; 32720 Rancho California Rd, Temecula • Vindemia Winery: Tasting $15-$20; Fri-Mon, 11am-5pm; (951) 760-9334; 33133 Vista Del Monte Rd, Temecula • For more wineries: TemeculaWines.org/taste

Dining Nearby

Windansea Beach

The Cottage La Jolla
(1.3 mi l 2 km away)
American • Breakfast, burger, salad, sandwiches, carne, seafood
$20-$40+ • ☑ Reservations • Sun-Mon, 7:30am-3pm; Tue-Thu, 7:30am-9pm; Fri-Sat, 7:30am-9:30pm • (858) 454-8409 • 7702 Fay Ave, La Jolla

George's at the Cove
(1.6 mi l 2.6 km away)
American • Burgers, pasta, sandwiches, carne, seafood, steak
$18-$100+ • ☑ Reservations • 11am-10pm; Fri-Sat, 11am-11pm • (858) 454-4244 • 1250 Prospect St, La Jolla

Del Mar Beach

Jake's Del Mar
(175 ft / 50 m away)
American ◆ Brunch, burgers, pasta, salad, carne, seafood, steak
$35-$75+ • Mon, 4pm-9pm; Tue-Thu, 11:30am-9:00pm; Fri-Sat, 11:30am-9:30pm; Sun, 10am-9pm • (858) 755-2002 • 1660 Coast Blvd, Del Mar

Pacifica Del Mar
(0.3 mi / 500 m away)
Seafood ◆ Brunch, mussels, salad, sandwiches, soup, seafood
$25-$75+ • ☑ Reservations • Mon-Fri, 11:30am-3pm & 5pm-close; Sat-Sun, 11am-4pm & 5pm-close • (858) 792-0476 • 1555 Camino Del Mar

Swami's Beach

Pannikin Coffee & Tea
(1.7 mi / 2.7 km away)
American ◆ Breakfast, coffee, tea, salad, sandwiches
$5+ • 6am-6pm • (760) 436-5824 • 510 North Coast Hwy 101, Encinitas

Union Kitchen & Tap
(0.2 mi / 350 m away)
American ◆ Flatbreads, salad, sandwiches, carne, seafood, steak
$25-$60+ • ☑ Reservations • Mon-Fri, 11am-9pm, generally; Sat-Sun, 9am-10pm • (760) 230-2337 • 1108 South Coast Hwy 101, Encinitas

*You ain't never
been in California?
Well, don' take my word.
Go see for yourself.*

– John Steinbeck

Notables Index

Abbot Kinney Boulevard, 63
America Tropical Mural, 86
Anaheim Ducks Hockey, 125
Anaheim Packing District, 126
Anza-Borrego Desert State Park, 134
Avila Adobe, 86
Balboa Park, 144
Bergamot Station Art Galleries, 71
Big Bear Lake, 47
Bradbury Building Foyer, 100
California Tower, 144
Cinespia, 44
Crystal Cove State Park, 125
Echo Park Lake, 46
El Rey Theatre, 56
Exposition Park Rose Garden, 92
'Extra Live' at Universal Studios, 20
Ford Amphitheatre, 37
Franklin D. Murphy Sculpture Garden, 71
Gamble House, 85
Grand Central Market, 102
Greek Theatre, 37
Griffith Park Observatory, 45
Hollywood Forever Cemetery, 44
Hotel del Coronado, 145
Huntington Beach, 124
Jimmy Kimmel Live!, 28
Joshua Tree National Park, 133
La Jolla Sea Caves & Reserve, 143
Lake Hollywood Loop Trail, 46
Laugh Factory, 55
Los Angeles City Hall, 101
Los Angeles Clippers Basketball, 92
Los Angeles County Museum of Art, 78
Los Angeles Dodgers Baseball, 93
Marina del Rey Harbor, 62
Melrose Trading Post, 29
Mission San Juan Capistrano, 124
Mulholland Drive, 46
NASA Jet Propulsion Laboratory, 92
Norton Simon Museum, 85
Olvera Street, 86
Original Farmers Market, 79
Palm Springs Aerial Tramway, 135
Palm Springs Air Museum, 135
Pantages Theatre, 29
Petersen Automotive Museum, 78
Point Mugu Sand Dune, 72
Ray Miller Trail, 72
Rodeo Drive & Golden Triangle, 78
Rooftop Film Club, 28
Santa Monica Pier, 62
Segerstrom Center for the Arts, 124
Silver Strand State Beach, 145
Sky Art of Borrego Springs, 133
Skybar, 28
Smorgasburg LA, 86
South Bay Coastal Trail, 62
South Coast Plaza, 124
Studio Tour at Universal Studios, 20
Surfrider Beach, Malibu, 72
The Broad, 100
The Comedy Store, 56
The Ellen DeGeneres Show, 19
The Groundlings, 56
The Roxy, 38
The Theatre at Ace Hotel, 101
The Troubadour, 39
The Viper Room, 38
The Wiltern, 102
Third Street Promenade, 63
Torrey Pines Gliderport, 143
Union Station, 86
Universal Studios Hollywood, 20
Univ. of Southern California Football, 93
Urban Kayaking on the LA River, 85
USS Midway Aircraft Carrier, 144
Venice Canal Historic District, 63
Virginia Robinson Estate & Gardens, 72
Warner Bros. Studio Tour, 19
Watts Tower, 85

Go. Adventure will follow!™

—

The YOLO Guide™
Los Angeles & Southern California

1st Edition

Copyright © 2017 Taj Bates
All rights reserved

The YOLO Guide™ is an imprint and
trademark of Striver's Row Press

ISBN 978-0-9974455-2-7

TheYOLOGuide.com

@theyologuide

No part of this book may be translated or reproduced in any form by any electronic or mechanical means, including photocopying, recording or information storage and retrieval without permission in writing from the author. Requests should be made in writing via TheYOLOGuide.com/contact.

This book is 100-percent unbiased. The author is not associated with and has not been compensated in any way by any of the vendors (companies, organizations, entities, etc.) detailed within—neither by direct payment nor in-kind gifts, products or services—in exchange for inclusion in this guidebook.

Vendor listings are informational and should not be viewed as direct endorsements by the author or publisher. All of the prices, fees, hours, services, etc., detailed herein are subject to change. The author and publisher do not assume and hereby disclaim any liability to any party for any loss or damage caused by errors, omissions or any potential travel disruption due to labor or financial difficulty, whether such errors or omissions resulted from negligence, accident or any other cause.

We welcome corrections and suggestions for the next edition of this guidebook, which can be submitted via TheYOLOGuide.com/contact.

—

PHOTO CREDITS—© Taj Bates, or public domain excepting the following: Brad Sutton/National Park Service; Rick Rowell/ABC Television; Ed Bierman; Andrew E. Larsen; Troy Williams; Joe Cooke; scrubhiker; Jon Viscott/City of West Hollywood; Greg Wilson; Wolfgang Puck Fine Dining Group; John Joh; T. Tseng; John Joh; Karlis Dambrans; CBS Television; Karlis Dambrans; Rick Rowell/ABC Television; Andreas Hub/Visit California; ABC Television; Celeste Lindell; Hollywood Bowl; Justin Higuchi; Justin Higuchi; Oliver Dodd; vxla; Rosa Menkman; The Academy of Magical Arts; The Academy of Magical Arts; The Comedy Store; Marc Cooper; Leyla Arsan; dirtsailor2003; chong chongchongchong; J. Paul Getty Museum; Marc Cooper; Harvey Barrison; Los Angeles County Museum of Art; Petersen Automotive Museum; Los Angeles County Museum of Art; Marika Bortolami; Army Corps of Engineers, Los Angeles District; Los Angeles Department of Transportation; Keith Allison; Sharon Mollerus; Scott Taylor; Los Angeles Philharmonic; The Broad; Justin Higuchi; Troy Williams; Shawn Ahmed; Shawn Ahmed; U.S. Navy; Paul Wirtz; Herbert Yu; Loren Javier; Sergei Gussev; Prayitno Hadinata; miguelb; chuck b; Alan Eng; Marshal Hedin; richmbythesea; John Farrell MacDonald; Tim Buss; San Diego Museum of Man; Kelly C.

www.ingramcontent.com/pod-product-compliance
Lightning Source LLC
Chambersburg PA
CBHW040328300426
44113CB00020B/2689